ANNIVERSARY EDITION

This special anniversary edition commemorates the 50th anniversary of the establishment of the California State Parks Department which is being celebrated throughout the State this year.

The State Parks system has been in existence 50 years, but this book pays tribute to a man who envisioned, and fought for, the concept of a "park" more than 27 years earlier. The vision and dedication of Andrew P. Hill resulted in the preservation of the redwoods of Big Basin as California's first state park.

Today other private individuals and organizations continue the work begun by Mr. Hill and his Sempervirens Club colleagues back in 1900. Sempervirens Fund, the modern-day descendant of Hill's original group, is still working to preserve parkland and redwoods in the Santa Cruz Mountains which Hill knew and loved.

This year marks the 10th anniversary of Sempervirens Fund as an active conservation organization. Coordinating closely with State Parks personnel, the Fund has added nearly 2300 acres of parkland to Big Basin Redwoods and Castle Rock State Parks and plans to acquire another 2300 acres for the two parks by 1980.

As we note Sempervirens Fund's 10th anniversary and the 50th anniversary of the California State Parks, we can pause to give thanks to Mr. Hill and the other foresighted men and women of his era whose concern and determination helped preserve much of the natural beauty we enjoy today. The impressive California State Parks system is their legacy and the redwoods their finest monument.

Claude A. Look
Executive Vice President
Sempervirens Fund

This book is No. 333 of a limited edition of 500 copies.

Grand and Ancient Forest

Andrew Putnam Hill
(taken about two years before his death)
(Courtesy of Sourisseau Academy, San Jose State University)

Grand
and
Ancient Forest

The Story of Andrew P. Hill
and Big Basin Redwoods State Park

by Carolyn de Vries

Carolyn de Vries

Fresno   Valley Publishers   1978

GRAND AND ANCIENT FOREST
Copyright © 1978 by Valley Publishers

All rights reserved. No part of this book may be reproduced or
utilized in any form or by any means without permission in
writing, except in the case of brief quotations embodied in critical
articles or reviews.

ISBN 0-913548-51-0
L.C. No. 78-50221

Published by Valley Publishers
Division of Book Publishers, Inc.
Fresno, California
Printed in the United States of America

For Bob, Karen and Greg
With all my love for their
support and understanding

*And out of the ground made the
Lord God to grow every tree
that is pleasant to the sight . . .*

Genesis 2:9

Trees of Enchantment; The Ever-Living

A group of nine people walked along the ridge between the two creeks. In the lead was their guide, and behind him the others followed in single file. One carried a large camera and tripod. Two of the nine were women and they wore long skirts, light-colored shirtwaists, and hats. A few carried staves in order to help themselves over this virtually trackless ground. Still, they went light-footed in anticipation, for they had been told of what they would find at their destination. Besides, it was May, and spring had come to the woods. The sun shone and there was beauty all around them.

The guide led them down off the ridge onto a large flat, where the shade was deep, and the forest ancient. Here they saw what they had come to see; and as they looked, they found themselves agape. It was more than they had dreamed of finding. They then walked in a trance; for it was a magic forest in which they stood, and it had cast its spell on them, a spell of which they would never be rid.

One it affected more than the others; his artist's soul was deeply stirred, and love flowed from his heart, while his mind dwelt on Creation. From that day onward, he belonged to the forest. His camera recorded its beauty, and his voice described its wonders. More than anything, he wanted it to live; so he gave generously of himself to persuade and work with others to save it from axe and saw.

Birdella Hill Laughlin

Acknowledgments

This research on the life of Andrew Putnam Hill and the beginning of Big Basin Redwoods State Park began in 1972, when as a graduate student in history at the University of Santa Clara, I was given permission to write my master's thesis on a local subject. Mr. Leonard McKay suggested that the life of Hill would be an interesting, and certainly worthy, subject for research. He introduced me to Mrs. Horace R. Laughlin, Hill's granddaughter. Mrs. Laughlin graciously opened her private collection of Hill papers and photographs to me, and as an added bonus, became a dear friend.

There are many people who should be thanked for their help during my research and it would be impossible to list them all here without the concern that some were forgotten. However, special friends who gave constant encouragement in this research must be remembered: Clyde and Helen Arbuckle; Theron and Frances Fox; Dr. Benjamin F. Gilbert, Professor of History, San Jose State University; Marian Lykken; Lynn Vermillion; and Austen Warburton. Also, the following organizations should be thanked for their cooperation in allowing the use of their photographs: Archives, University of Santa Clara; San Jose Historical Museum; Sempervirens Fund, Inc.; Sourisseau Academy for California State and Local History, History Department, San Jose State University; and Sunnyvale Historical Society and Museum Association.

Portions of this manuscript were used in my article entitled "Andrew P. Hill and the Big Basin, California's First State Park," which appeared in the November 1976 issue of *San Jose Studies*.

Carolyn de Vries

Table of Contents

Waddell Creek with Big Basin in the background.
(Courtesy of Sempervirens Fund, Inc.)

Introduction

Champions of Conservation

For decades man has given the appearance of being intent on destroying, in the name of progress, those things which were created for his benefit and pleasure. John Muir, the foremost American naturalist and conservationist, put it succinctly when he wrote, "Any fool can destroy trees. They cannot run away; and if they could, they would still be destroyed—chased and hunted down as long as fun or a dollar could be got out of their bark hides, branching horns, or magnificent bole barkbones."[1] It was just this kind of outcry that was needed to stir the conscience of the American people. Through Muir's efforts, a drive was initiated which culminated in Yosemite being set aside as a state park in 1864. In 1890 it was transferred to the federal government, as were Sequoia National Park and General Grant Grove.

From 1869 to 1914 John Muir traveled the Sierra. The American people learned of the conservationist's journeys as a result of the narratives he wrote concerning his travels. His fervent pleas stressed the need to save the scenic natural beauty of America. Although his ideas were not unique, American western development was in a period in which wilderness was still an obstacle, a barrier in the battle for civilization. Unlike many of his contemporaries, John Muir saw this vast wilderness as worthy of salvation. His descriptions of the American scenic-beauty that he sought to save were, while poetic to the ear, designed to stir the conscience of the American people:

The forests of America, however slighted by man, must have been a great delight to God; for they were the best he ever planted. The whole continent was a garden, and from the beginning it seemed to be favored above all the other wide parks and gardens of the globe. To prepare the ground, it was rolled and sifted in seas with infinite loving deliberation and forethought, lifted into the light, submerged and warmed over and over again, pressed and crumpled into folds and ridges, mountains, and hills, subsoiled with heaving volcanic fires, ploughed and ground and sculptured into scenery and soil with glaciers and rivers—every feature growing and changing from beauty to beauty, higher and higher. And in the fullness of time it was planted in groves, and belts, and broad, exuberant, mantling forests, with the largest, most varied, most fruitful, and most beautiful trees in the world.[2]

To Muir, the only practical way to preserve this beauty was through conservation, for which he became the country's chief spokesman. In 1892 he helped found the Sierra Club. The members of the club, academicians as well as businessmen, felt the need for the preservation of America's natural beauty, and although its original purpose was the conservation of Yosemite Valley's wilderness, the members quickly became the defenders of many wilderness areas throughout the United States.

As Muir and his associates continued their fight for wilderness conservation, the political winds of the nineteenth century began gradually to change in favor of the Sierra Club's goals. The West settled, the barriers surmounted, the conservationists found defenders in politicians who began to favor protective legislation and the creation of government reserves over blatant exploitation of American forests. Conservation grew in popularity. The preservation of natural resources rather than exploitation for private gain became a popular philosophy. Organizations such as the Association for the Advancement of Science and the American Forestry Association, aided by Muir's club, promoted the ideas of conservation that led to the later establishment of the Division of Forestry within the already existent Department of Agriculture.

The new organizations encouraged a rapid acceleration in the acceptance of conservation ideas. John Muir was no longer alone in his quest for conservation. Gifford Pinchot was one who shared Muir's ideals. A man of wealth who had studied at the National School of Forestry in Nancy, France, Pinchot became America's first native-born professional forester. Within the conservation philosophies of Muir and Pinchot lay the beginnings of the two primary schools of conservation thought of the nineteenth century, and the seeds that were soon to develop into the conservation ideas of Andrew P. Hill, artist, photographer, a man in quest of nature's beauty.

The year 1895 brought an interest in Big Basin's already oft-threatened redwoods. Leland Stanford, former United States Senator and founder of Stanford University, considered the purchase of several thousand acres in the Big Basin area as a botanical preserve for the university. Although the preliminary survey of the area proved to be highly favorable, the Senator dropped the idea when he found the price for the land to be more than he was willing to pay.

Although the Basin did not gain a supporter in Stanford, it finally found its Muir, in the year 1900, in Andrew Putnam Hill. Hill became the generative force that brought forth Big Basin as a redwood park.

An unpleasant experience with the owner of the Felton Big Trees Grove, Joseph Welch, in 1899, was all the impetus Hill needed to become a full-time, active conservationist. His main goal in life became the preservation of the redwoods through the establishment of a park, and, although discouragement plagued him often, his strong determination and genius for organization made possible the achievement of that goal. This book is the documentation of that accomplishment.

On May 27, 1934, the San Jose *Mercury Herald* retold the story of the fire in the Santa Cruz Mountains which led Hill to begin his movement to save the coast redwoods. (Author's Collection)

The Early Years

Andrew Hill was one of the most ardent supporters of Big Basin Redwood Park. The conservation of the Basin's redwoods became his life's passion, and although at one time he questioned the neglect of his family and business for such a cause, he never abandoned the magnificent trees. Instead he followed the advice of Judge A. L. Rhodes of San Jose who was reported to have told Hill: "You are a comparatively young man. Make it your life's work to save these trees. You can do nothing greater for your country."[1] The need to help conserve the redwoods was not something Hill had always felt. It developed gradually over the years, as do most goals.

A growing awareness of the artistic beauty of nature during Hill's early years probably helped to shape and direct the conservation goal that characterized his later years. A look at those early years will show those events which prefaced the development of the one most important aspect of his life.

Andrew Putnam Hill was born August 9, 1853. His family, which had settled in Pleasant Township, a small hamlet in Porter County, Indiana, had an intense pride in its ancestral heritage. Throughout his childhood Andrew listened to many tales of the accomplishments of his forebears. The men in his family had received heroic acclaim for their activities in both the American Revolutionary War and the War of 1812, and their stories created in the young Andrew a sense of pride that remained an important part of his life. It was still apparent in 1917 when he wrote to one of his sons:

My Great Grandfather on my Mother's side fought in the Revolutionary War; my Grandmother's Father was Drum Major to Washington's staff. My two Grandfathers were in the War of 1812; my Uncles were in the Mexican War, and in the Rebellion. I was 9 years old but saw a battle. Guess it is *in the breed*.[2]

Hill was an only child. His grandfather, Elijah B. Hill, had obtained land in Cuyahoga County, Ohio. His father, Elijah Putnam Hill, had moved from Ohio to Indiana as a young man and was a buyer of furs for the Hudson Bay Company for a time.

In April of 1850, at age twenty-eight, Elijah Putnam Hill married Jane A. Rose, who was affectionately referred to as Jenny. Her father, Henry Montgomery Rose, had also been a member of the fur trade. He had moved to Indiana before 1850, leaving the fur business for the plowshare.

It must have been a few months before Andrew's birth that Elijah left his young wife in Indiana while he traveled by ox train to California. While crossing the plains, he and a fellow traveler, Sam Manning, were detailed to round up stock which had been run off by Indians. They became separated from the train and were attacked by more hostile Indians. They barely survived a twenty-four-hour battle, which left them bone-weary and physically weakened, barely able to make their way to Amador City, California, a small gold rush town about forty miles southeast of Sacramento. Seven days later, the young Elijah was dead as a result of the strain and exposure to which he had been subjected.

In 1851, two years before Andrew's birth, Jenny Hill's brother, Albert H. Rose, had left Ohio for California. He arrived in San Francisco, and shortly afterwards made his way to the rich gold fields of Fine Gold Gulch in Fresno County and then to the placer deposits along the banks of the American River. His time in the gold fields was brief, however.

Andrew Putnam Hill in the year of his arrival in California. He was 14. (Courtesy of San Jose Historical Museum)

Within a year of his arrival in California, he moved to Amador City, married, started a family, and became a significant investor in mining and real estate ventures. He campaigned successfully for the State Senate seat of Amador and Alpine Counties in 1865. His business activities concerning the Keystone Mine later came under suspicion, and he lost his claim to ownership in spite of a struggle that went as far as the office of the Secretary of the Interior.

In 1867, when Andrew was fourteen, he and another of his mother's brothers, H. Warner Rose, went to California by way of the Isthmus of Panama. They stopped at Amador City, and within a year Andrew entered the small College of Santa Clara, a Catholic school in Santa Clara. Though not a Catholic, he studied there for two years, one in the "preparation department," the equivalent of high school, and one in "second division." His strongest memory of those two years was of the earthquake of 1868. In later years, reminiscing about the incident, he recalled that that earthquake equalled in force the one

3

Santa Clara College as it looked in the 1860s, when Andrew attended its high school. (Courtesy of Sourisseau Academy, San Jose State University)

of 1906. To him, the rise and fall of the earth seemed like the swells of the ocean. It was soon discovered that, as a result of the quake, the brick walls of the chapel were no longer safe. The students helped in pulling them down, a process which also required the removal of several bodies which had been buried in the church. Hill was present when the tomb of the founder of Santa Clara College, Rev. Nobili, was opened, and he recalled in later life that though the remains were skeletal, the brown bones of the hands still held a crucifix.

In 1870, young Andrew left Santa Clara College and went to San Luis Obispo to work on the ranch of his uncle, H. Warner Rose. He had worked for his uncle only one season when his childhood interest in art was aroused by an opportunity to learn the techniques used in map making. While studying this art form with a corps of engineers, he made the acquaintance of Charles Reed. Reed, at that time a resident of Yolo, California, had studied engineering at West Point and was best known in the West as the engineer of the Fremont expedition of 1846. Reed quickly recognized Hill's natural ability and encouraged the young man to improve his talent through lessons.

Hill followed Reed's advice and in 1875 traveled to San Francisco to enroll in the California School of Design. The art school was new to the city, having been founded in February of 1874 by the San Francisco Art Association. Hill studied techniques of drawing the human figure with a renowned Italian painter of nature, Virgil Tojetti. He also studied under other teachers, among them Louis Lussier, with whom he later worked professionally.

By 1875, Dr. Hugh J. Glenn, "The Wheat King of the World," had become known because of his huge harvest of wheat and the "Monitor," the machine that harvested his land in the Sacramento Valley. George Hoag, a machinist on the Glenn Ranch, had built the "Monitor" and "in its day, [it] was the pride of the Sacramento Valley."[3] That same year Andrew Hill was commissioned by Hoag to paint "the world's record harvest scene of Dr. Glenn and his crew threshing with the machine 'Monitor.'" He journeyed up the Sacramento River to Jacinto to paint "A California Harvest Scene," a four by five-foot canvas which depicted men, machine, mules and horses cutting and threshing wheat. While there, Hill saw the crew set a new one-day world's record. Eighty-four men and 130 draft animals threshed and garnered 6,183 bushels of grain. The painting was Hill's first commission as an artist and the beginning of his growing involvement with nature and art.

One year later Hill formed a partnership in a portrait painting business with Louis Lussier, his former instructor. During that year he lived in San Francisco. He spent 1877 in Oakland, and in 1878 he took up residence in San Jose, where he taught art classes and operated a portrait studio. By then the twenty-five-year-old painter's talents had become well known to the public. His work on life-size portraits of Governor William Irwin, ex-Governor Romualdo Pacheco and Senator Newton

Booth was reported in an article in the *Daily Alta California* dated February 5, 1878.

It was during this period also that he painted two of his large works, "The Murphy Party" and "Mission Santa Clara." The former was an historical painting showing the first emigrant party to ascend the Sunset Pass from Donner Lake in 1844. This painting won a gold medal at the California State Fair in 1890 for best oil painting in landscape and was purchased and placed in the historical room of the Society of California Pioneers. It was destroyed in the 1906 earthquake.

Hill and Lussier returned to San Francisco as partners in 1880. Two years later Lussier died, but Hill remained in the city for another year. It was probably at this time that he began work on "Camp of Israel," a monumental painting sixteen by forty feet, commissioned by J. W. Ketchner of New York. Hill described this painting as

... showing the camp of the Israelites before Mt. Sinai, when Moses received the law. This work contained a representation of more than 25,000 tents, which were pitched in such a way that every tent faced the holy of Holies. It also showed thousands of figures, dressed in the peculiar Egyptian styles of that period as described in the Holy Bible. The Oriental colors were particularly pleasing. It was exhibited at the Young Men's Christian Association at Brooklyn, New York in 1900. The New York Journal published an engraving occupying two pages and gave a graphic account of the picture.[4]

Although Hill's passion for art filled much of his life, he did not devote all his time to the brush and pallet. He met, courted and finally married, in April of 1883, Florence Maria Watkins, a local San Jose woman. Benjamin Watkins, Florence's father, a native of Genesee County, New York, had joined the ill-fated Donner Party on its westward journey in 1846. Fortunately for Watkins, and also for Andrew Hill, indirectly, he left the

Andrew Putnam Hill as a young man. (Courtesy of San Jose Historical Museum)

wagon train at Fort Hall and proceeded safely to Oregon and later, in 1847, to San Francisco. His decision to leave the Donner Party saved him from probable death and allowed him to return to the East in 1850 to marry Laura Broughton, who later bore him eight children. The couple left the east coast soon after their marriage and traveled back to California and the Santa Clara Valley, where Watkins became one of the first in the area to plant orchards and nurseries.

On January 8, 1857, Laura Watkins gave birth to a daughter, Florence Maria. A Santa Claran by birth, Florence grew up in the city, and attended San Jose Normal School, graduating in 1876. Before her marriage she taught school for eight years, "a talented member of the school department." She was a "young lady of many accomplishments of mind and person" as well, and her social standing and natural talents were an asset to Andrew Hill's growing career.

Within ten months of their wedding date, the Andrew Hills announced the birth of their first child, a son. It was a joyous event, but their happiness was short-lived for the baby died of "shock" on February 6, 1884, just three days after his birth. The young couple was deeply grieved, but two years later that grief was lessened by the birth of a second son, Andrew Putnam, Jr., on June 4, 1886, and two years following, on August 29, 1888, a third son, Frank Ernest.*

Hill continued his career as an artist with his studio located on North First Street in San Jose. He still dabbled heavily in nature scenes, such as "Bridal Veil Falls," painted in 1884, perhaps an early indication of his later leanings toward conservation. He also painted portraits and ranch life scenes. Although his painting kept him busy, he was unable to draw an adequate living from it, and so, encouraged by his wife and the need to provide for two growing boys, Hill ventured into the art of photography.

---

*Both boys spent considerable time during their childhoods at Big Basin. Each was to excel in his chosen profession. Andrew, Jr., graduated from Stanford University as an architect but spent most of his life in the field of education. Before his death in 1973 and after his retirement as the head of the Stockton School District, he became the resident manager in Stockton of Mutual Fund Associates, whose main office was in San Francisco. Frank also graduated from Stanford University, receiving both a Bachelor's and Master's degree in English literature. He taught at Stanford and at Columbia University before becoming an editorial writer for the New York *Globe*. He was later Literary Editor of the New York *Sun* and then joined the publishing house of Longmans, Green, where he was editor-in-chief. Interested in the writing of both poetry and prose, he concentrated in later life on these endeavors. He died in 1969.

*Hill's wife, Florence, with their two sons, Andrew Putnam, Jr.,
and Frank Ernest.* (Courtesy San Jose Historical Museum)

In 1889, Andrew Hill and J. C. Franklin entered into a
business partnership, Hill and Franklin Photographic Studio
and Art Gallery. Franklin left the partnership within a year and
Hill, with financial backing from his mother-in-law, established the business of Hill and Watkins. In 1892 he formed a
third partnership, with Sidney J. Yard, an Illinois artist and
photographer who had received his training in England. This
partnership endured for three years, during which time the
photographers captured much of early Santa Clara County on
photographic plates. For two of the three years that the men
worked together they operated a branch gallery in Palo Alto.
The opening was noted in the local paper, the Palo Alto *Times:*

Mr. Andrew P. Hill, our artist photographer, now
comes to Palo Alto regularly on Tuesdays, Thursdays and

Saturdays. This week he is having the gallery here painted, inside and out. The inside will be finished in a delicate flesh tint, which has been found to produce the best effect in the way of light in taking a photograph.[5]

Hill and Yard possessed a rather large collection of photographs of the area. Numbered among them were pictures of Mt. Hamilton, Stanford University, the Stanford horses, and Santa Clara County. Hill's photographs of the horses owned by Senator Leland Stanford were taken over an eight-year period and in 1901 were used to illustrate a *Sunset Magazine* article on "The Horses of Palo Alto."

Photographs from the studios of Hill and Yard were part of the Santa Clara County display at the World's Columbian Exposition in Chicago in 1893. Hill's work was mentioned in the Palo Alto *Times* at several times. Among the occasions covered by the paper were his visit to the Sherwood Hall Nursery to photograph the flowers in bloom, and his climb to the top of Wilson's tank to take photos of the business section of Palo Alto. However, financial trouble developed for the firm of Hill and Yard in 1894, and by October of that year it was necessary for the partners to declare "voluntary insolvency" and dissolve their business association. Yard moved to Carmel, and Hill remained in San Jose to try again on his own.

His new photography studio was located in the Porter Building on the corner of Second and Santa Clara Streets. His business advertisement described him as being a "portrait painter and photographic artist." During the first year of this new venture, Hill was commissioned to take photographs for the publication, *Santa Clara County and Its Resources, A Souvenir of the San Jose Mercury*, popularly called *Sunshine, Fruit and Flowers*. Outside his photography studio, Hill also formed a partnership with William Yeaton. The men established a poultry brokerage at 313 Willow Street, San Jose. All types of purebred poultry were bought and sold on commission.

Andrew Putnam Hill at about age 37. (Courtesy of Sourisseau Academy, San Jose State University)

In 1898 Hill again moved his painting and photography studio, this time to the Safe Deposit Building located at First and Santa Clara Streets. In addition to his usual work, he sent over three hundred photographs to periodicals throughout the world; as usual, his most frequent subjects were people, animals and landscapes. An article written about him at this time stated:

> ... people insist on his making their portraits and secure his services in getting striking views of their residences, property and animals. Mr. Hill is an enthusiastic admirer of fine poultry owning some of the best, and some of his most difficult work has been to get just the right pictures of birds that won't stand still, and won't show off their good points except when no camera is around.[6]

By the time Hill was commissioned to photograph the redwoods for *Wide World Magazine*, his business had increased tremendously. He was called on to illustrate many periodicals and until his work for Big Basin took most of his time, he was able to continue with other work as well. President McKinley's visit to California prompted the publication of a book for which Hill took the photographs. Also, beginning in 1900, his illustrations appeared in rapid succession in *Out West, Overland Monthly, Sierra Club Bulletin*, and *Sunset Magazine.* While many of these articles were about the redwoods, Hill also published photographs of San Jose, Boulder Creek, the Stanford horses, and the Passion Play at Santa Clara College.

Although much of Hill's early life was spent in travel and business problems, the conservation seed had been planted and was being nurtured by his paintings and photographs of the natural beauty that so strongly drew him for subject matter. Awed by the beauty of the Big Basin, he began to feel the first stirrings of a desire to see the majestic giants preserved for future generations. How much this desire was to dominate his life he probably couldn't have guessed then.

The Priceless Heritage

The Big Basin redwoods have stood for many centuries, and their magnificent beauty and majestic grandeur have impressed many a passerby. However, near the end of the nineteenth century, the area's value was not in its beauty but in the prize timber yield that it offered. High quality redwood found a market not only in California but in other states as well. Redwood proved to be excellent construction material and there were many who would willingly have sacrificed the redwood's natural beauty for the profit the lumber would bring. Andrew Hill, appalled at the proposed destruction of the trees, turned his efforts toward initiating a campaign that would ensure the preservation of the Big Basin's redwoods. Their beauty was a national asset too valuable to lose.

Although a few people had warned of the growing scarcity of coast redwoods, the first partially successful effort to save the trees began with editorials in 1886 and 1887 by a Redwood City newspaperman, Ralph S. Smith. As editor of the Redwood City *Times-Gazette*, he sought to awaken general interest in the desirability and necessity for the government to acquire redwood forests for posterity. In one editorial he listed four reasons why the redwoods of the Big Basin area of the Santa Cruz Mountains should be preserved as a park: the unique beauty of the trees; the closeness of Big Basin to the population center, San Francisco; that the trees should not be in private ownership; and that logging was not profitable to the area because of its inaccessibility.

Hill's photo of Lick Observatory on top of Mt. Hamilton.
(Courtesy of San Jose Historical Museum)

In a follow-up editorial Smith stated that while he realized all coast redwoods could not be saved, those in the Big Basin area should be because of their still-virgin state.

Support for Smith's idea came from both the Santa Cruz *Sentinel* and the San Francisco *Chronicle*. Duncan McPherson, editor of the *Sentinel*, expressed his interest in a park in the Big Basin. And the *Chronicle* published an article entitled "A Redwood Park," which noted the beauty of the redwoods and the desirability of parks in general. The article included the information that twenty thousand acres could be purchased for about fifteen dollars an acre.

During the week of July 5, 1887, Smith met with the State Board of Forestry and suggested that the Big Basin be set aside as a park. No action was taken at this meeting, and some people claimed that Smith's interest in the redwoods was stimulated by the desire of the Spring Valley Water Company to secure permanent cover for their Pescadero watershed. The rumored connection between Smith and the water company was never proven; in November of 1887 Ralph Smith was killed. His death, perpetrated by an irate reader, brought doom to the

LICK OBSERVATORY.

A typical advertisement for 1890, the year Hill received financial backing from his mother-in-law, Laura J. Watkins. (Courtesy Sourisseau Academy, San Jose State University)

proposal for a park. There was no one interested enough to pursue Smith's ideas.

The movement to create a park in the Big Basin area remained dormant until 1889 when Captain Ferdinand Lee Clark, a well-known retired military man visiting the Santa Cruz area, became interested in the redwoods. In an article in the Santa Cruz *Surf*, he wrote of his plans to set aside thirteen hundred acres in the Big Basin as a game preserve and "great redwood park":

> ... All the underbrush on the plateau of Waddell Creek of 300 or 400 acres will be cleared away and a great redwood park will be opened. Fourteen men are now clearing for a road. It is expected the place will be swarming with hunters and fishers.[1]

Disputes over land titles, however, forced Clark to give up his idea for a game preserve. Nevertheless, his interest in the redwoods did not cease when his business venture fell through. He continued to write articles for both the San Francisco *Chronicle* and the San Jose *Mercury Herald* encouraging recreational use of the area. His new idea for a public redwood park was editorially supported by the *Chronicle*. Clark continued his work in the Basin area and as a result helped to arouse a renewed interest in the Basin, but lack of political or commercial support forced the park project to be tabled for a while.

Hill's interest in the trees had started soon after his arrival in California in 1867. He listened intently and with awe to the stories and descriptions of the redwoods and was fascinated by the wildlife that lived in the Basin area—the huge California grizzly bear, the mountain lion and the timid deer. Although the Basin was dense with heavy undergrowth and in some areas even inaccessible to man, Hill was not deterred from exploring as much of it as he could. His artistic nature was attracted by the grandeur of the enormous trees, which he loved to paint.

In the fall of 1899 there had been a fire in the redwoods behind Wright's Station, a small community in the Santa Cruz Mountains. One of the local vineyards had been saved from destruction by men dousing the fire with wine which was aging in tanks at the vineyard. This unusual method of fire-fighting aroused much interest, and a London magazine, *Wide World*, assigned Professor C. F. Holder, president of the California Academy of Sciences, to write an account of it. In order to illustrate his article, which was entitled "How a Forest Fire Was Extinguished with Wine," Holder asked Hill to photograph trees in the coast redwoods area. In a letter to the magazine (and also in the article), Holder wrote:

> The entire fire was the most terrible experience which this part of California has ever passed through. I directed Mr. Hill to take a photo of one of the large redwoods to show the size of the trees in the Santa Cruz Mountains. The owner objected, despite the fact that it was for an English magazine; but Mr. Hill persisted so you have the tree [sic].[2]

Another version of the story stated that Hill had to pay an entrance fee to the Felton Big Trees Grove to take his pictures.

The Peabody School in San Jose, c. 1896. (Courtesy Sourisseau Academy)

Alameda School in San Jose, c. 1896. Hill's photos of all Santa Clara County schools have helped in the tracing of their histories.(Sourisseau Academy)

17

As the owner, Joseph Welch, was away at the time, Hill waited for his return to ask questions about the time when General Fremont had allegedly lived in a hollow tree on the property. When Welch returned he was most disturbed to discover that Hill had taken photographs, maintaining that no one was allowed to do so as his hotel sold souvenir pictures to tourists. Not only did he refuse to give information about the General Fremont tree, he also demanded Hill's photographic plates. Hill, angered, would not give them up. However, the plates quickly diminished in importance when Welch told Hill that he planned to fell the magnificent redwoods for railroad ties and firewood.

If Hill was not an active conservationist before that, he certainly became one then. His resolve that the trees must be saved began to grow at that moment, and it was with firm determination that he waited for the San Jose train at Felton Grove that spring day:

I was a little angry, and somewhat disgusted, with my reception at the Santa Cruz big trees. It made me think. There were still fifteen minutes until train time. Just as the gate closed, the thought flashed through my mind that these trees, because of their size and antiquity, were among the natural wonders of the world, and should be saved for posterity. I said to myself, "I will start a campaign immediately to make a public park of this place."

I argued that as I had been furnishing illustrations for a number of writers, whom I knew quite well, that here was a latent force which, when awakened to a noble cause, would immediately respond, and perhaps arouse the press of the whole country. Thus was born my idea of saving the redwoods.[3]

A fellow traveler on the train ride was an old acquaintance of Hill, San Jose attorney John E. Richards, who also wrote articles for the San Jose *Herald*. Richards listened to Hill's experiences with Welch at the Felton Big Trees Grove and agreed that the redwoods should be saved. After proposing to write articles for the *Herald*, Richards immediately started on the task while Hill wrote a letter to his good friend, Josephine McCrackin, telling her of the situation and asking her to write something for the Santa Cruz *Sentinel*. When the train pulled into Wright's Station, Hill handed his letter to Mr. McCrackin, who habitually met the train, to give to his wife, and the campaign was on. Josephine McCrackin's article appeared March 7, 1900 in the *Sentinel*. She wrote of the persistent discourtesy that Hill had encountered and remarked: "I am not acquainted with Mr. Welch, but I think we all agree with Mr. Hill when he says that the course this gentleman takes is utterly un-American; and I add that it is un-Californian." Richards' article was published that same evening in the San Jose *Herald*. People in the immediate area could no longer be unaware of the danger to California's coast redwoods.

On March 17, 1900, just ten days after interest in saving the redwoods was so excitingly revived, an editorial in the Santa Cruz *Surf* noted that since Congress was preserving the Big Trees of Calaveras, it seemed an opportune time "for the revival of the agitation instigated some years ago in behalf of a redwood preserve." The editorial asserted that the situation seemed to be a case of "now or never with the Big Basin," and reminded people that this area was the last possible reservation of redwoods that included not only big trees but also the varied growth once found in typical California forests. The preservation of Big Basin, the editorial pointed out, seemed to be "nobody's business." Readers were reminded that in two years the area would be devastated by the timber-cutters.

Hill continued with his plans for saving the Felton redwoods by writing letters to the Santa Cruz *Sentinel*. An article by him appeared in that paper April 3, 1900 entitled "To Save the Giant Redwoods." Hill also corresponded with the Boards of

IN CALIFORNIA'S GARDEN

SANTA CLARA VALLEY

Opposite page and photo right are pages of a publicity brochure telling of Santa Clara Valley. It was written in 1897 by Carrie Stevens Walter, who later was most helpful in garnering support for the establishment of Big Basin State Park. Andrew Hill took most of the photos for this publication. (Author's Collection)

Trade (both later known as Chambers of Commerce) of both Santa Cruz and San Jose, requesting them to pass resolutions asking Congress to purchase the redwood trees for a public park. The resolutions were passed and the San Jose body appointed John E. Richards and Mrs. Carrie Stevens Walter, along with Hill as chairman, to a standing redwood committee.

Almost immediately Hill was urged by J. F. Coope, Secretary of the Santa Cruz Board of Trade, to plan for a public meeting to "crystallize sentiment" and encourage positive action for saving the trees. Coope felt it would be preferable to hold such a meeting away from Santa Cruz and so Hill was asked to make the arrangements. He proposed, "in order to shut out any possibility of politics," to seek the cooperation of educational institutions, and with this in mind he consulted Dr. David Starr Jordan, president of Stanford University. Jordan agreed with the plans and the word went out that a meeting of people interested in saving the redwoods would be held at the Stanford University Library, May 1, 1900.

The Alameda, c. 1890, one of Hill's best known photos. (Author's Collection)

Amid considerable publicity, the meeting was attended by Dr. Jorden, who presided; Stanford professors W. R. Dudley (botany), J. M. Stillman (chemistry), Charles B. Wing (civil engineering), and R. L. Green (mathematics), who also represented the Sierra Club; Professor J. H. Senger of the University of California; Professor John J. Montgomery of Santa Clara College; Professor James McNaughton, president of San Jose Normal School (now San Jose State University); ex-Governor William T. Jeter; F. W. Billings and J. Q. Packard from the Santa Cruz Board of Trade; John E. Richards; Mrs. Carrie Stevens Walter; and Andrew P. Hill of San Jose.

Just prior to this meeting Hill had received another letter from Coope, telling him of a suggestion made by Dr. C. L. Anderson, a botanist living in Santa Cruz, that the people at the meeting should consider the acquisition of the Big Basin instead of the Felton Grove, as the former contained larger trees in a much larger area which would be most suitable for a park. Anderson was supposed to have told the Santa Cruz Board of Trade, "As your enthusiasm is for these smaller trees, so will it grow in proportion to the size, the grandeur and the vastness of those in the Big Basin." When Hill talked to Dr. Jordan, he was told that Stanford professors Dudley, Marx, Smith and Wing had already explored the Big Basin region and had made maps and a survey of the area, and that the professors were very much in favor of a public park there.

The suggestion to save the redwoods in the Big Basin, instead of those at Felton, became the primary consideration at the Stanford meeting. A survey committee was appointed to go into the area and report on the suitability of the Big Basin as a park site. Since only Hill and Mrs. Walter were not "too busy" to serve on the committee, they were made responsible for selecting others to join them.

On May 15, Hill, Mrs. Walter, W. W. Richards, R. S. Kooser and Mrs. Louise C. Jones started their journey to Big

Hill's photo of a prominent San Jose real estate firm, James A. Clayton & Co., in 1895. (Courtesy of San Jose Historical Museum)

Hill's photo of the San Jose Box Factory. (San Jose Historical Museum)

Basin. The reconnoitering party went by train from San Jose to Boulder Creek and from Boulder Creek to the end of the road by horse-drawn vehicle. They were joined in Boulder Creek by their guide, Andy Baldwin, a cook, Thomas Croon, J. F. Coope and J. Q. Packard from Santa Cruz, and Charles W. Reed of the San Francisco Board of Supervisors.

Somehow the members of the committee had been able to interest H. L. Middleton, largest stockholder in the Big Basin Lumber Company, in joining their exploration for a short time. It had been discovered that one of the mills owned by his company had packed machinery on mules over the mountains to the very rim of the Big Basin, close to some of the largest trees, and was ready to begin cutting.

...Mr. Middleton was dragged, willy-nilly, along with the camping party, and held as friendly hostage while his woodchoppers cut trails in any direction that was suggested. For the first time the extent of the Basin was fully realized, and the value of the watercourses, the Waddell,

24

May 1, 1900 meeting at Stanford University for conservation-minded citizens. Left to right, J. H. Senger, David Starr Jordan, W. R. Dudley, F. W. Billings, James McNaughton, J. Q. Packard, William T. Jeter, John E. Richards, Carrie Stevens Walter, J. M. Stillman, Charles B. Wing, John J. Montgomery, R. L. Green. Hill photo. (Courtesy of Sourisseau Academy)

the Gazos, the Pescadero Creek, the Butano, all taking their sources here. Days were spent in exploration; and before the party went back to civilization . . . Mr. Middleton had become inoculated with the spirit of this redwood-saving crowd . . . [4]

During their exploration of the Big Basin, the committee walked farther and farther into the forest. As they emerged into the opening before a redwood which towered over three hundred feet in height, Hill noticed "the members of our party all looking at this giant with open mouths, and suddenly I became aware of being in the same condition!" Their awe increased as they went on their way.[5]

Although Hill was a member of the Basin party, concerned with the preservation of the woods, one of his other functions was to photograph much of the scenery that the group encountered. Engrossed in his camera and his subject, Hill became separated from his companions on May 17. Believing him to be completely lost, the group sent out word, and the next day both the Santa Cruz and San Jose newspapers reported the "mysterious disappearance" of Hill to their readers. Fortunately, he had found his way back to the camp, safe but hungry, almost before the papers were printed. The editor of the Boulder Creek *Mountain Echo* visited the party at its camp to check on the details of Hill's disappearance.

When shown Santa Cruz and San Jose papers with the sensational accounts of Mr. Hill's being lost, they laughed long and loud over the ridiculousness of the whole affair. All agreed that it was not every man who was fortunate enough to live to read his own obituary . . . In spite of the veracious and multitudinous newspaper authority at hand, Mr. Hill and his associates insisted he had never been lost at all, but slept comfortably every night in his tent at Camp Sempervirens.[6]

It was around the evening's campfire on May 18 that Hill suggested the formation of a forest club to preserve the Big Basin. J. F. Coope named it "The Sempervirens Club of California." They passed the hat and collected $32 to help in the costs of their campaign. Later, as the club became more firmly established, the members adopted the motto "Save the Redwoods" and listed as their objectives: to save the redwoods for posterity; to save the trees and many species of fauna in the area for scientific study; and to create a park for all people to enjoy. The first officers of the club were Charles W. Reed, president; Carrie Stevens Walter, secretary; J. Q. Packard, treasurer; W. W. Richards, sporting secretary; and Andrew P. Hill, official artist. Fifty prominent citizens of California were appointed honorary vice-presidents.

Sempervirens Club members spent the next few months enlisting supporters for their cause. Their organization was expanded to include members in San Francisco and throughout

Exploration party at Big Basin, May 15-19, 1900. Left to right, Louise C. Jones, Carrie Stevens Walter, J. F. Coope, J. Q. Packard, Andy Baldwin, Charles W. Reed, W. W. Richards, and Roley Kooser. Hill photo.
(Courtesy of Sourisseau Academy, San Jose State University)

central California as well as in San Jose and Santa Cruz. They secured "vigorous newspaper support" as well as backing from such groups as the Native Sons and Native Daughters of California, the Sierra Club, and the California Pioneers of Santa Clara County. Enthusiastic response was forthcoming, but "the real, living force working with and through the club came from the universities of Stanford and California and the college of Santa Clara."[7]

On May 27, 1900, the San Francisco *Chronicle* printed a long article supporting the purchase of the Big Basin, including photographs by Hill. The Boulder Creek *Mountain Echo* reported on articles concerning the issue which had appeared in the Stockton *Independent* and the San Jose *Mercury*, stating that the *Mercury* felt that the Big Basin should be out of local control and politics and suggested federal control of the park. Support was also forthcoming from the American Association for the

Advancement of Science, the American Forestry Association and the Society for the Promotion of Agriculture.

A most important step in the preservation of the Basin was taken when Hill, Dr. Jordan and Professor Dudley of Stanford met with H. L. Middleton, the lumberman who had visited the Sempervirens in their camp. Middleton proved himself eager to help save the redwoods by assisting the men in obtaining an option for one year on 14,000 acres in the Big Basin area.

In August 1900, the *Overland Monthly* printed an article, "About the Big Basin," written by Josephine Clifford McCrackin and illustrated by Hill. The author described the worst enemy of the redwoods not as fire, as one would imagine, but as "the greed, the rapacity, the vandalism that would hack and cut and mutilate the grandest, the most magnificent forest that can be found on the face of the globe." She urged everyone to join in the effort to preserve the trees, and referred to Yosemite and Yellowstone as playgrounds for the wealthy only. Ending the article was the reminder:

> There are four sawmills at work over there now, eating their way into the heart of the timber—grinding, grinding, grinding, not slowly as do the mills of the gods, but swiftly and surely, as demons and destruction always work.[7]

With the formation of the Sempervirens Club of California, Big Basin had found its Sierra Club, and in Andrew P. Hill its John Muir. Like Muir, Hill could not stand idly by and watch the sawmills destroy the redwoods; the campaign to save the trees had begun!

A Park Is Born

The site of the second meeting of the Sempervirens Club, on July 3, 1900, was the Palace Hotel in San Francisco, a setting quite different from the one of that first informal meeting around a campfire. The members authorized a government agent from the Bureau of Forestry to represent their interests in Washington, D.C., but on August 5 they met again and decided to appeal to the California Legislature instead of the United States Congress for a park. This decision was apparently made because the Sempervirens felt that an appeal to Congress to purchase the Big Basin might jeopardize the passage of another bill already pending to purchase the Calaveras Big Trees in the Sierras. Also, there was reported opposition in Washington to the purchase of any park lands by the federal government. That same week in August, the Boulder Creek *Mountain Echo* reported that Eugene F. Loud, United States Congressman from California, was most emphatic in his opposition to creating more parks.

The Sempervirens also decided at their August meeting to send representatives to the upcoming political conventions of California with the hope of persuading at least one of the parties to include the purchase of the Big Basin in its platform. These efforts were apparently unsuccessful as the newspapers did not mention anything about state acquisition of Big Basin during their many months of reporting on the political campaigns.

After the elections in November 1900, the Sempervirens again pushed for the creation of a park at Big Basin. The club met in San Francisco to plan the campaign for the proposed park and announced that it was confident of raising $100,000 for the purchase. Charles W. Reed, appointed by the club's members, authored the park bill that was presented to the California Legislature for action. Printed in an illustrated folder by the Sempervirens Club, the bill proposed the creation of the "California Redwood Park." Assemblyman George H. Fisk of San Francisco introduced the bill, A B 200, in the Assembly on January 15, 1901. The bill required the creation of a Redwood Park Commission which would include the Governor and four executive appointees, to select

land in the State of California upon which are growing trees of the species known as 'sequoia sempervirens,' and which, in the judgment of the said Commission, is most suitable for a park whose purpose is to preserve a body of these trees from destruction and maintain them for the honor of California and the benefit of succeeding generations.

After locating the site, the Commission was to purchase it for not more than $500,000 or else obtain the land through condemnation rights. The bill as introduced asked the legislature for $250,000 of the amount needed.[1]

Following the preparatory state printing, the bill passed into the hands of the Committee on Public Lands and Forests. Hearings were held at which several people from Santa Cruz appeared to speak in favor of the purchase of a redwood park. At another meeting of the Committee, speeches favoring the park were heard from Professor William Dudley of Stanford University, Rev. Robert E. Kenna, S.J., President of Santa Clara College, and Charles W. Reed and Mrs. E. O. Smith of San Jose. On January 30, 1901, the Committee voted approval of the bill and sent it back to the Assembly with a "do pass" recommendation. As the bill required expenditure of state funds, it was next sent to the Assembly Ways and Means Committee for review. This committee, perhaps considering the expenditure to be foolish, returned the redwood park bill to the Assembly floor on February 8, 1901 with a "do not pass" recommendation.[2]

The Sempervirens quickly held another meeting in San Francisco in February of 1901. Some members were willing to give up the idea of a park for the Big Basin area. Hard work had not gotten them anywhere and they could see no prospects for a change in the feelings of the legislators about the project. But Andrew P. Hill refused to give up, believing the bill could still be passed.

> His enthusiasm aroused hope in some, and provoked ironic smiles from others, but to all it seemed fitting that he should take charge of the cause that he refused to believe was lost.

Being unanimously elected as a committee of one, Hill left for Sacramento carrying as many of his photographs of the Big Basin as he could.[3]

Hill first sought the advice of Lieutenant Governor Alden Anderson, a former San Josean. Anderson suggested several changes in the bill that would help it go through the Ways and Means Committee, of which he was a member. He also advised Hill to seek help from a well-known politician, Grove L. Johnson, father of Senator Hiram Johnson. Armed with his photographs, Hill went to Johnson and persuaded him to sponsor the bill. Johnson had the bill reported back to the committee, where it was rewritten. This second version spread the acquisition of the land over a five-year period, specified definite boundaries for the proposed park, and required a title search by the State Attorney General before purchase. Following its return to the Assembly floor, the bill received a favorable recommendation.

But passage of the bill was not yet in sight. Hill learned that a "push"—a group that accepted bribes for favorable votes on

The Palo Alto Times *marked the 71st anniversary of the movement to save the redwoods on May 17, 1971.* (Author's Collection)

certain bills—controlled the California Legislature and that $5,000 was required to arrange for the passage of the redwood park bill. Although he had already made many friends in the legislature who would vote favorably, Hill felt that more votes were needed to ensure the bill's passage without the $5,000 bribe. Since the Catholic members of both the Assembly and Senate constituted a rather large minority in the legislature and their voting record in the past indicated that the members usually voted together, he decided to seek the Catholic votes for his park. He asked the aid of his good friend, Rev. Robert E. Kenna, S.J., President of Santa Clara College, hoping that the priest would be able to sway not only the Catholic legislators but Catholic congregations throughout the state. Aware that the congregations could influence the Catholic legislators, he asked Rev. Kenna to arrange an opportunity for him to speak at a meeting of the Society of Jesus. At the meeting Hill requested that a committee be appointed by the Society to visit Big Basin before deciding on the merits of the park issue. The committee returned with enthusiasm and the desire to influence other Catholics to support the park bill by mentioning it in sermons and church announcements.

Meanwhile, D. M. Delmas, a San Francisco attorney and noted orator, was requested by the Sempervirens Club to visit the proposed park area and then address the California Assembly on February 18, 1901. In his speech Delmas named two often-heard objections to the park purchase: that the owners were wealthy and should donate the land for a park, and that the price was higher than the commercial value of the land. His answers to these objections were that the owners were not willing to donate the land and lose the income from it, and that the state would be buying virgin redwood, not cut timber. He also reminded the legislators that the countries of France and Germany as well as the states of New York and Massachusetts had set aside funds to purchase forest lands and that California should do the same. Delmas was foremost an "actor" and as he bore a "striking resemblance to Napoleon" would cultivate this resemblance by his posture and a lock of hair across his forehead.[4] It was in this pose, no doubt, that he said:

> Man's work, if destroyed, man may again replace. God's work God alone can re-create. Accede, then, to the prayers of the people. Save this forest. Save it now. The present generation approves the act; generations yet unborn, in grateful appreciation of your labors, will rise up to consecrate its consummation.[5]

The March 2, 1901 issue of the Boulder Creek *Mountain Echo* reported that Hill was still at work trying to save the redwood park bill. The bill was to be submitted on March 3 as A B 873. As changed earlier, it now specified the Big Basin as the area for the park.

The many legislators who did not want to approve the park purchase were able to place a new and urgent condition on their favorable votes: that the Sempervirens Club had to obtain a new option on the Big Basin area to keep the loggers out while the state completed purchase. Hill immediately went to San Francisco and met with H. L. Middleton, the representative of the timber owners who had helped before. The one condition the owners wanted for extending the option on the land was a guarantee of $50,000 to be paid to them in case the state should fail to make the first payment on time. Hill promised to have that guarantee by midnight of the same day. Taking a train south, he called that evening on President Jordan of Stanford University, but Jordan was unable to help. Hill then went to Rev. Kenna at Santa Clara College. Rev. Kenna was able to obtain the guarantee of $50,000 from his nephew, James Phelan, a man generous to many such causes. Hill telephoned Middleton from Santa Clara with the news that the condition of the timber owners could be met.

Hill's photograph of the San Jose visit of President Theodore Roosevelt in May 1903. (Courtesy of Sourisseau Academy, San Jose State University)

And yet, Hill was still not able to rest that night. In order to show the legislators some proof that the new option had been secured, he decided to seek help from Harry G. Wells, editor of the San Jose *Mercury*. Since the streetcars did not run at that time of night, Hill had to walk from Santa Clara to the offices of the *Mercury* in San Jose, a distance of four miles. Arriving about 1:00 A.M., he asked Wells to write an editorial telling of the accomplishment. As the paper had already gone to press, Hill was able to convince Wells to run off a special edition of 150 copies in which Hill himself wrote the editorial. Because he needed to have the newspapers on the desk of every legislator for the morning session, he caught the 4:30 A.M. milk train to Sacramento.

When bill A B 873 was again called up for reading, most of the legislators had read their newspapers with the front page editorial announcing fulfillment of the conditions set for passage. After hearing speeches by Assemblyman G. S. Walker of Santa Clara County, George G. Radcliff of Santa Cruz County, and H. W. Brown of San Mateo County, the Assembly passed the California Redwood Park bill with a vote of fifty-five in favor and one against.

Now the bill was ready for the California State Senate. Rev. Kenna had followed Hill to Sacramento and he spent the day talking to various legislators brought to him by Hill. Even after the Assembly passage of the bill, a poll of Senators showed only seven in favor of the park. Just before the Senate adjourned, Senator Charles M. Shortridge of San Jose, at Hill's request, asked the legislators to stay and listen to Rev. Kenna. Of the occasion, Rev. Kenna later wrote:

> My remarks, though very simple, were given with an earnestness that made the Senators accept them as the sentiments of my heart. I said in part: "Senators, I do not come to speak to you as a priest, nor as the president of a great college, nor in the language of such, but as a 'forty-niner,' and in the language of one who loves the great land of the West, and her magnificent forests which so often charmed my boyhood days and thrilled my young heart with high and noble aspirations. They spoke to me of Liberty, and they filled the mind with great thoughts and the soul with lofty aspirations. These redwoods are pre-eminently Californian, unique in their species and situation, and as a forty-niner I beg you to stay the hand that would harm those that still remain to recall the glories of those vast virgin forests now no more."[6]

When the Senate vote was taken, the California Redwood Park bill passed almost unanimously. The lone vote in opposition came from the chairman of the Finance Committee who was in favor of the bill but felt he could not conscientiously vote for such a large expenditure.

Even after the passage of A B 873 by both the Assembly and Senate, problems were encountered. Governor Henry T. Gage, given two forestry measures for signature, had to make the decision to sign both, which was highly unlikely, or to veto one. One measure was for the creation of a forestry and irrigation commission to plan a comprehensive policy of forest and land protection, the other for the creation of a state park in the Big Basin. Governor Gage could sign only one of the bills if he were to uphold his party's stand on excessive government spending. Also, the forestry commission bill had wide political backing and many legislators later said they voted for the Big Basin park bill only because they considered it a dead measure.

Hill again went into action. He had long before used up the money given him for expenses by the Sempervirens Club, and his own personal funds were negligible. By economizing his resources, moving to a cheaper room, and eating at a laborers' lunch counter for fifteen cents a day, he was able to budget enough for one final effort. Sending telegrams all over the state, he asked supporters of the California Redwood Park bill to send letters and telegrams to Governor Gage urging his signature on the bill. Also, a public hearing was set up by Governor Gage and the Sempervirens Club. Advocates for the park attended from all over the state. Speaking for the scholars and scientists were Professors William Dudley of Stanford and J. H. Senger of the University of California. Both scholars sought the preservation of the park area as a natural wilderness. Professor Dudley was strongly in favor of the park because of its unlimited value as a botanical garden. If the Basin were designated as a state park, protected from loggers and developers, it could still be utilized by Stanford students as a natural study area.

Professors Dudley and Stenger were joined by the Native Sons and Native Daughters, the California Pioneers, and representatives from local Women's Clubs. Like Hill, they all looked upon the Basin as worthy of preservation by virtue of its natural beauty, and like John Muir, Hill and his associates believed that the primary purpose of conservation was to conserve God's creation in its natural state. Although they acknowledged the value of the forest products that the Basin offered, they could not accept even controlled logging as Pinchot had advised in the nineteenth century. While the Pinchot plan would have replaced the trees that were cut down and would have utilized careful management of the area's natural resources, the loss of just one of the magnificent redwood giants was an idea impossible for the park's supporters to accept. Even though, in years to come, Hill would accept the partial development of the Basin, he was unwilling at this point to give an inch. Their adversaries were strong, but Hill and the park's supporters would not accept defeat.

Governor Gage was faced with the decision: the public wanted him to sign the redwood park bill while the politicians wanted him to sign the forest and irrigation commission bill. To help make the decision, the Governor asked the advice of Dr. Jordan, who argued in favor of the Big Basin park bill, pointing out that the forestry commission bill could wait, while "any delay in connection with the proposed [park] might be fatal."[7]

With overwhelming public support behind him, Governor Gage signed the California Redwood Park bill on March 16, 1901, stating, "now poor and rich alike might enjoy the pleasures of these grand groves of nature."[8]

Hill and his associates had succeeded! The park was now a reality. The popularity of the bill's passage was acclaimed by the newspapers of California. A spokesman for the American Forestry Association stated:

> In this act California has not only done a great service to the cause of forest protection in the United States, but has also given her citizens a superb park for the enjoyment of themselves and their posterity . . . [9]

When President Theodore Roosevelt, himself a great conservationist, visited California in 1903, he said at Stanford University on May 12:

> ...the interest of California in forest protection was shown even more effectively by the purchase of the Big Basin Redwood Park, a superb forest property the possession of which should be a source of just pride to all citizens jealous of California's good name.[10]

Andrew P. Hill was also praised for his dedication to the park project. A reception by the San Jose Woman's Club was held in his honor just a few days after passage of the bill. However, while San Jose was busy giving tributes to Hill, a few people elsewhere were concerned lest they get none of the credit. The Santa Cruz *Surf* printed several editorials on the subject reminding locals of the work done by people in Santa Cruz County, and in one editorial quoted Assemblyman George S. Walker as he indignantly wrote of the praise being "wasted," stating "at least twelve men were responsible for this bill, and any one of them failing to do what he did do would have caused the defeat."[11] Although a few people were anxious to steal the credit from Hill, members of the Sempervirens Club were well aware that, if it had not been for Hill's untiring efforts, there would be no California Redwood Park.

During an outing to Big Basin by the Sempervirens Club in 1901, several trees were named. The first was the "Santa Clara Tree," in honor of Santa Clara College, whose president and alumni had taken such an active part in helping to secure Big Basin as a state park. Some of the people pictured are Nell Fenton, Rev. Michael McKay, S.J., Rev. Robert Kenna, S.J., Miss Royce, Mrs. Fremont Older, Carrie Stevens Walter, Florence Hill, Mrs. Woods, Mr. Castro, Young Fenton, and Jeremiah Cunningham. (Courtesy of Archives, University of Santa Clara)

Guardian of Big Basin

While the Park Commission was becoming a reality, Hill continued to photograph the Big Basin. His photographs remained the primary source of illustration for the numerous articles, written by various authors, that continued to fill magazines and local newspapers. When the Pan-American Exposition opened in Buffalo, New York in May 1901, among the exhibitions were Hill's photographs. One in particular caught the attention of all who saw it. Eighteen feet long and almost two feet high, it was a panoramic view of more than forty of the redwood trees in the proposed park area. This picture had required the printing of thirteen negatives side by side on a continuous roll of photographic paper.

> . . . . in order to do the printing in this way Mr. Hill had to invent and manufacture a special printing frame with rollers at each end for printing a continuous picture. The effect is that of a continuous forest of giant redwoods. It falsified nature only to the extent that these various groups of giants, standing in the forest at various distances of fifty to several hundred yards, are brought together in a continuous line.[1]

The technique was unique and produced one of Hill's most dramatic pictures.

Meanwhile, Governor Gage appointed four members to serve with himself on the Redwood Park Commission: William H. Mills, land agent for the Southern Pacific Railway Company; Arthur W. Foster, regent of the University of

Original entrance of the state redwood park at Big Basin.
(Courtesy of Sempervirens Fund, Inc.)

California and President of North Pacific Coast Railway; Rev. Robert E. Kenna, S.J., President of Santa Clara College; and Dr. William R. Dudley, head of the Botany Department at Stanford University. An advisory board of five men was also appointed to help the Commission in its labors. It was the duty of these men to investigate the Big Basin area and to bargain for and buy the best land possible for the $250,000 allocated to them by the legislature.

The Commission worked slowly, however, and disagreements arose regarding the price of the land. Commissioner Mills maintained that the price of $100 per acre was too much and that the Big Basin area was largely inaccessible. In spite of popular public opinion in favor of the creation of a park, the expenditure of state funds by a party elected on a platform of moderate government spending might produce negative feelings among that same public, a result not welcomed by the party.

Although the future creation of the park had been made possible by legislative action, the bill by which this was done had never had full backing by many of the legislators and had been voted in favor of by many only so that it could be removed from the calendar. A number of those who supported it had done so believing that it would be vetoed by the governor. Even some of the men who had been appointed to the Commission did not envision a redwood park as enthusiastically as did Hill, and felt that the land for the park should be donated to the state by the lumber companies.

The San Francisco *Call*, supporting Mills' opinion, was blasted in an editorial in the Boulder Creek *Mountain Echo*. Both the *Mountain Echo* and the San Jose *Mercury* favored the creation of the park and in their editorials maintained that the *Call* had at the very least been inspired and probably had been paid by those hostile to the park to take such a stand. As the *Echo* reported in August 1901:

> ...much of it [the *Call*'s reporting] is absolutely false, while the other portions are that half truth, which is the worst kind of a lie, because not so easy of refutation. It is very [un]pleasant indeed for those public spirited and noble men and women who have worked so hard to have this giant created where the people may enjoy this marvelous forest forever, to have their motive impugned and their characters attacked by one of the leading newspapers of the State, regardless of whether it was done for pay or merely to make a sensation.[2]

This issue was solved when experts visited the area and were able to convince the Commission that the amount of standing timber was much larger than supposed, thus making the land worth even more than the $100 per acre asking price. Also, the

Redwood Park Commissioners and Advisory Board visited the park in September 1901. Left to right, General Chipman, J. F. Coope, Prof. W. R. Dudley, W. H. Mills, Harvey Lindley, Rev. Robert Kenna, S.J., Governor Henry Gage, unknown man, John Green (guide), Duncan McPherson, the steward, and unknown man. (Author's Collection)

area had become more accessible because of the milling operations nearby.

An added problem developed when the time limit on the land option secured a year previously by Hill, Jordan and Dudley expired. An extension was requested by the Sempervirens Club amid rumors that the original timber owners might start logging the proposed park site. The club obtained a renewal of the option for a period of two months, but at the end of that time the owner of 320 acres of land within the Big Basin, I. T. Bloom, grew tired of waiting for the state to purchase the land, and proceeded to cut his timber.

News of the logging at Big Basin no doubt inspired the Commission to act as quickly as possible. Hill obtained permission from H. L. Middleton to invite Governor Gage and the members of the Park Commission to examine personally the proposed park site. Several small cabins and a cook house were erected at the site later known as "Governor's Camp." For the building of these structures, lumber had to be packed on mules for two and a half miles beyond the end of the trail. The Governor's party of six joined Hill and other members of the Sempervirens Club at the Big Basin area known as Slippery Rock. A stage had brought them to the Basin from Boulder Creek, but they viewed the redwoods from horseback.

Shortly before the governor's trip, Hill was able to arrange for members of the Sempervirens Club and other interested persons to camp in the redwoods for ten days, in August of 1901. Tents were erected at Slippery Rock, and Jacob Overton, an ex-slave who had settled in San Jose, cooked for the group. A few of the campers, W. W. Richards, Mrs. Louise C. Jones and Edwin S. Williams among them, returned home to write glowing reports of their days in the redwoods. Later, Josephine McCrackin published an account of the trip in *Western Field*. She described Andrew P. Hill not only in his official capacity as artist and photographer for the group, but as their "Columbus" as well for "he discovered the Big Basin." Although this was not an accurate statement, it probably did sum up the feelings of her fellow members of the Sempervirens Club. They knew of Hill's dedication to the project better than others. McCrackin's article also recorded first impressions as the group wandered among the trees:

> Even those among us who were far-traveled and world wanderers still found something to admire and marvel at here; far as the eye could reach there was grandeur and sublimity . . . . Tape measure and camera were in such constant use; fresh discoveries of strange plant growth, of flower and shrub, of beautiful forest vista and forest trail, were so frequently made that time and distance seemed annihilated . . . .[3]

The success of the adventure led to another one like it the following summer. Nearly fifty people joined Hill on these outings.

Sempervirens Club campout in Big Basin in 1901.
(Courtesy of Sempervirens Fund, Inc.)

On July 23, 1904, Dr. Hugo de Vries, a noted botanist from Holland, accompanied members of the Sempervirens Club camping in the Big Basin. Later de Vries was to write of the efforts of the movement to save the redwoods:

> The Californians commenced to realize that they were bordering the loss of one of Nature's greatest wonders, which has become the fame of the state of California, and which has added so greatly in the state's wonderful development.[4]

A year after gaining the approval of the California Legislature, the Redwood Park Commission finally purchased 2,500 acres of prime redwood for $250,000 and was given 800 acres of chaparral and 500 acres of cut-over or burned land capable of reforestation. Originally designated California Redwood Park, the area continued to be known locally as Big Basin and was officially given the name, Big Basin Redwoods State Park, in 1927.

Following the purchase of the park, the Commission appointed J. H. B. Pilkington of Santa Cruz as Warden and invited campers to use the area. Warden Pilkington and his coworkers were the first to sight the forest fire that began on September 7, 1904. The fire started during the hottest day of the year in a sawdust pile near Waterman's mill, and for twenty days the "midday sun was a ball of fire in a bank of smoke." Before rain quelled the blaze, the fire had swept over three canyons and creeks and cut a swath from one to three miles wide all the way to the ocean shore; approximately 1,200 acres of the park burned. Only the eastern border of the park suffered damage; the central and western portions remained unharmed. One of the redwoods in the Basin smoldered with fire for fourteen months; the remaining portion of this tree still stands in the park today.

While the park had survived the worst of the forest fire, it was still threatened by politics and the lumberman's axe. On March 18, 1905, the California Legislature abolished the Redwood Park Commission and placed Big Basin under the charge of the State Board of Forestry, a group composed of the Governor, Secretary of State, Attorney General, Secretary of the State Board of Examiners and the State Forester. The result was to remove control of the park from the direction of educators and private citizens and place it in the hands of politicians. As these public officials had other duties to perform, in actuality the State Forester became the sole manager

Camp Sempervirens at Big Basin.
(Courtesy of San Jose Historical Museum)

of California Redwood Park. In 1907 a new state administration replaced Warden Pilkington with S. H. Rambo, a State Senator from Boulder Creek.

Political control of the park was exercised with less enthusiasm than that provided by interested citizens, and soon after the changeover rumors of the park's demise began to circulate. It was a newspaper article that first warned of the cutting of trees in Big Basin. An article in the September 14, 1907 issue of the Boulder Creek *Mountain Echo* stated:

> State Forester Lull has let a contract for removing all dead and fallen trees and decayed timber in Redwood Park, with the aim in view of improving the appearance of the reserve. He states that an impression has gotten out to the effect that his plans for the improvement entail the setting up of a shingle mill within the confines of the Park, for the purpose of making shingles of the timber that is to be removed. The report is not correct. The forester says he would not permit a mill or anything of the sort to be constructed in Redwood Park.

Throughout the following few months, messages were sent to Hill from friends in Boulder Creek warning of the cutting of good as well as burned timber in the park. Alarmed, Hill called a meeting of the Sempervirens Club for January 15, 1908, in San Francisco. At that meeting the Sempervirens appointed their secretary, Alexander Murgotten, to visit the Big Basin and report his findings. A San Francisco newspaper reported Hill's saying: "No stone will be left unturned to keep the Redwood Park as nearly in the primeval state as possible."[5]

Murgotten was joined by a representative from the Native Sons of Watsonville, and their report confirmed that scores of live redwoods as well as burned timber were being converted into grape stakes, posts, pickets and shingles. Two days later a photographer visited the area and the Santa Cruz *Surf* published pictures of the devastation. Other newspapers in the area published similar articles in an attempt to make the public more aware of the situation. Resorting to familiar tactics, in February 1908 Hill turned to the San Jose *Mercury* to inform Californians of what was happening. He described a visit to the Basin by a joint committee made up of representatives from the very groups that had been instrumental in securing the passage of the park preservation bill. The committee, which included Hill, called upon Warden Rambo and were assured that only burned redwoods and some dead pine or fir were being cut. The next morning they began their investigation, only to find at Sempervirens Camp a woodyard of pickets and posts and split timber covering acres of ground:

> Here we saw many beautiful green redwood trees, the cleanest, largest and best specimens in this part of the Park, alive, unburned, with green leaves upon them, cut down; some all cut into wood or posts but the stumps, others half cut, and so on . . . . This terrible devastation of the people's forest; this awful slaughter of live, beauti-

Evidence of timber cutting in Big Basin in 1907.
(Courtesy of San Jose Historical Museum)

ful trees, embraces many acres of this section of the Park, and in its awfulness is beyond my description with the pen ... [6]

A few days later the Santa Cruz Grand Jury met and took action. The decision required that all cutting be stopped but allowed the contractor to remove from the park redwood that had already been felled. After this incident the California Legislature restored the Redwood Park Commission, which once again became representative of the educational institutions and public-minded citizens. Control of California Redwood Park remained under this Commission until the park became part of the State Park System in 1927.

Writing later of the scandal, Dr. William R. Dudley said:

This incident of the legalized but wholly objectionable lumbering in the Park shows the people of this peninsula that the price of its most attractive natural feature is eternal vigilance, and not simply the $250,000 that was paid over from their state treasury.

In March 1908 Andrew P. Hill became president of the Sempervirens Club, continuing in that position until his death in 1922. The welfare of the park tended to dominate Hill's life although he continued his painting and photography studio for the support of his family. Even as disaster entered his business life, in the form of an earthquake which totally destroyed his studio, Hill remained undaunted in his role as guardian of Big Basin.

The 1906 Earthquake
and Its Aftermath

The headlines in the San Jose *Mercury* on the morning of April 19, 1906 told a grim story of an earthquake and fire the day before. One article was carried under the terse heading: "Dougherty Building Completely Gone and Other Buildings Must Be Torn Down." For four years prior to that day, the studio of Andrew P. Hill had been located on the top floor of the Dougherty Building. The disastrous fire which followed the quake burned all his paintings and photographic plates that were stored in the studio. Writing in a letter to the California State Library less than a year later, Hill told his own story:

> Although it has been some 35 years since I commenced painting, my life has been one of many interruptions, and I have not yet achieved what I have sought . . . I suddenly lost by fire on April 18th last all of the studies of a lifetime and many paintings of more or less merit.

Summing up the work that was lost, he told of two years work already done on a painting of the laying of the cornerstone of Stanford University. It needed only eight months more to finish and contained eighty-six portraits of prominent men of the time who had witnessed the ceremony. Stating that this could never be replaced, he added the comment, "all burned without insurance with all the sketches of a lifetime."[1] There is no question that this catastrophe had a lasting effect on the lives of Hill and his family.

Prior to the earthquake, Hill had continued to maintain his studio while actively engaged in the creation of the park at

Florence Watkins Hill in Hill's studio, c. 1904.
(Courtesy of Sourisseau Academy, San Jose State University)

Big Basin. A humorous episode in Hill's life as a photographer was recorded by Franklin Hichborn, a chronicler of the California Legislature. In the year 1901, President David S. Jordan of Stanford University had shocked many local people by driving a two-seated automobile from San Jose to the summit of Mount Hamilton. A few months later a local car salesman, Colonel Cotten, boasted that he could make the same trip within twenty-four hours instead of the two days required for Jordan's trip. Cotten placed a substantial wager to back his boast. One of the conditions of the wager was that a photographer should accompany the group to take a picture of the automobile with four passengers in it in front of Lick Observatory on Mount Hamilton. Hill was chosen. Two automobiles made their way up the mountain: the first one carried Colonel Cotten, the driver, a prospective customer, a local physician (in case of accident), and newspaper reporter Hichborn; Hill followed in the second car with two more prospective customers and a driver.

Before we reached the city limits so many horses had been frightened, that the Colonel when he saw a horse coming would stop until the animal got by, but even then there were near run-aways. When a young lady out for her morning ride on a rather spirited animal found her horse getting out of control, the doctor, Cotten and myself [Hichborn] leaped to her assistance. With some difficulty we led the trembling animal out of sight of the machine. Hill got a picture of us. It showed Cotten's machine, the frightened horse, and the three heroes rescuing the endangered lady.

Continuing on their journey, the cars traveled at a speed of ten miles per hour. Even at that speed it was noon before they got to Smith's Creek at the foot of the mountain. As there was a restaurant nearby, arrangements had been made in advance for the group to lunch there. Hichborn commented that he had made the journey with horse and buggy in much less time. While at the stop one of the drivers put gasoline into the first car while Hill and Hichborn looked on. Feeling that there was more than enough gasoline already in the car to "blow us all to kingdom come," Hill told the driver that he would take care of filling the second car, but instead he poured the gasoline on the ground. Halfway up the mountain the second car chugged to a stop, and it was soon discovered that the gas tank was empty. With some gasoline from the first car, the second managed to get as far as 200 feet from the summit before it stopped again. There the passengers had to disembark and push the machine the rest of the way to the summit. Hill took his picture of the feat just before sunset and also confessed to what he had done with the gasoline. By this time he was an unhappy man, and when Hichborn asked him what he thought of automobile travel, he replied, "If I get back to San Jose alive, I'll never ride in one of these pesky things again."[2]

After the disaster in 1906, Hill no longer maintained a studio in town but worked out of his home at 1350 Sherman Street, San Jose. The home was a typical one of its day, with bedrooms on one side of the hall and parlors and kitchen on the other. Canoas Creek ran across the back of the property and, although the house was built high off the ground, it still experienced a few floods. Most of the surrounding land was planted in fruit trees and vegetables which elicited high praise during the World War I "victory garden" craze. Near the back of the garden was a cottage made into a studio and darkroom. It was this studio that would house Hill's work until his death.

In 1907 Hill sought other ways to recuperate his financial losses. Earlier in his life he had bought stock in a gold mine in Calaveras County, and now he decided to spend some time in an attempt to develop it, hoping for a profitable return, not only for himself, but also for a few friends he had persuaded

Dougherty Building, which housed Hill's studio, after the 1906 earthquake and fire in San Jose. (Courtesy of San Jose Historical Museum)

to invest in the mine. Feeling responsible for their investments and hoping to increase the heretofore meager returns on them, Hill took over as president of the Ingomar Consolidated Gold Mining Company in 1910. Although the mine was a mile northeast of the town of Campo Seco in Calaveras County, 175 miles from San Jose, Hill took an active part in its management until his death. His diary for 1911 makes several references to the mine. On one particularly exciting day he wrote, "Struck copper on first blast!"

By September of 1911, however, work had ceased, and although other attempts were made to rework the mine, by 1917 it had become apparent that sale of the mine would be the only way to salvage the invested money. Hill's wife, Florence, mentioned the mine in a letter to their son Frank that same year:

Andrew is at the mine, with a second party. His first "prospect" did not buy saying it would take too large a sum to equip and develop the mine. Well, I do not depend upon the sale very strongly, so my disappointment will be less, if it does not go thru.[3]

The sale was not made, and when work was started again at the mine, Hill supervised it once more.

In a letter written early in 1918 to his son, Hill said:

Well the mine took me to the City today and I blew in a whole day trying to get something out of the mine. We are going to drive on one the old Fay Tunnel, and extend the crosscut of the Mexican ledge. Curnow [a worker at the mine] says they missed it 22 feet, and a survey proves it. So we are hoping with all of our strength for something to happen favorable. It has with others, why not with us?[4]

The Ingomar Consolidated Gold Mining Company never brought to Hill the financial success he had hoped for. In the early part of 1922, his unprofitable work for Big Basin, in addition to family illness, made it necessary for almost half of the family's shares in the mine to be sold. The sale of the company did not take place until several years after Hill's death.

Earthquake, fire, or mining operations did not sway Andrew Hill from his interest in Big Basin. The solace he found among his beloved redwoods may have been the greater for him because of his involvement in projects concerning the park—or perhaps those projects offered a kind of solace, too. One of the projects concerning the park which was undertaken by the Sempervirens Club when Hill was president was a petition to the United States Congress asking that 3,200 acres of unoccupied government land in the Big Basin be deeded to the state to become part of California Redwood Park. Bill No. 18277 was introduced by Congressman E. A. Hayes and Senator George C. Perkins, both local men. Its passage added ten scattered parcels of land to the park.

A second project, which required nine years to complete, resulted in the construction of a road into the Big Basin from the Santa Clara County side. Hill launched this undertaking early in 1906, collecting $800 from friends to pay for a survey of the proposed route. The survey was made, but the earthquake intervened and the project had to wait until Hill was again able to take time from his own affairs to devote to it.

By 1910 the proposed road from Saratoga summit into Big Basin was taking a considerable amount of Hill's time. He sent circulars to interested persons and groups, encouraging donations of time and money with the statement, "We ask you to help us in this because it is the right thing to do."[5] After he learned that the Panama-Pacific Exposition would be held in San Francisco in 1915, Hill's desire to open the park from the Santa Clara County side increased. He gained encouragement and inspiration for this project from his long-time friend, Rev. Kenna, who shortly before his death in 1912 wrote in a letter to Hill:

> It is a crying shame that this great primeval park of the state has for ten years been practically ignored so far as real development and opening it to the public is concerned. The little that has been done . . . has not been in any way real work for the development of the Park for the whole people, which we want, and must have, if possible, by 1915, when, we trust, we shall have good roads into the park, and a magnificent boulevard through it, so that the people of the old world, coming over by the million, may be shown over a grand state highway through this primeval redwood park.[6]

Three times the California State Legislature had passed a bill appropriating money to build the road, only to have it vetoed by three different governors. Believing that the upcoming 1915 exposition would add impetus to the project, in August 1912 the Sempervirens launched a new campaign. When a committee from the club, including Hill, went to Sacramento to appear before various committees of the legislature, they had nine bound volumes of petitions signed by some 43,000 voters to present. Their efforts were also assisted by Redwood Park Commission members Professor Wing of Stanford University and the Rev. James P. Morrissey, S.J., new President of Santa Clara College, who appealed to the legislature for the bill's passage.

The bill had been written by Senator Herbert C. Jones of San Jose and was introduced by Senator William R. Flint from San Benito County. It provided for the "survey and construction of a state highway from Saratoga Gap...to, into and within California Redwood Park in Santa Cruz County," and made appropriation of $70,000 for the project. It did not, however, provide for the purchase of a right-of-way along the route and stated that no work could begin on the road until a strip two hundred feet in width was deeded to the state. When the bill was approved June 7, 1913, the problem of the right-of-way was left to Hill and the Sempervirens Club. Hill called on his many friends, including such California notables as James L. Flood, James D. Phelan, A. B. Spreckels, W. H. Crocker, and W. H. Cowell, and collected the sum of $7,602, which was used for the purchase of all the remaining rights-of-way along the route of the proposed road.

A gala banquet was held by the Sempervirens Club in San Jose just a few days after the passage of the Saratoga Gap road bill. Four people were singled out for laurels during speeches by notables at the gathering: Josephine Clifford McCrackin, the Santa Cruz County writer whose articles had told of the plight of the Big Basin; the late Rev. Robert E. Kenna, who had served on the Redwood Park Commission and had been an inspiration to the club's efforts; Professor William R. Dudley of Stanford University, who had given so much of his experi-

Advertisement for Hill's studio located in the ill-fated Dougherty Building which was destroyed in the 1906 earthquake. (Courtesy of San Jose Historical Museum)

ence and advice to the project; and Andrew P. Hill, who was named "the foremost figure, night and day, in the movement." When Hill himself rose to address the group, he was given "an ovation that seemed to come straight from the hearts of the assembled guests." In his speech, Hill acknowledged the help and support which had been given by the newspapers of California, particularly the San Jose *Mercury*, which had published some 400 articles about Big Basin written by Hill. Expressing his thanks to all who had come to the banquet, Hill said:

> This has not been a one-man's fight nor a one-woman's fight. It has been a fight of organizations of the people of California; they have worked like a team...[7]

On May 10, 1915, the Sempervirens Club of California sent a letter signed by Andrew P. Hill, President, and Alex P. Murgotten, Secretary, to all members and friends:

> Please make immediate preparations to attend the Panama-Pacific Exposition on Tuesday, May 18, 1915, to help the Sempervirens Club of California celebrate the completion of the new State Automobile Road from the Saratoga Summit to the California Redwood Park.

The festivities at the Exposition began in the afternoon with a parade to the California Building, escorted by Exposition officials and a military band. Hill's address at the gathering included a short history of the founding of the Sempervirens Club and its work for Big Basin. Summarizing the accomplishments of the club, he cited the initial appropriation of $250,000 from the state for the purchase of 3,800 acres of forest land; the ceding to the state by Congress of lands within the Big Basin; the appropriation of $70,000 for the construction of the road from Saratoga Summit; and the raising of $7,602 in private subscriptions for the purchase of a right-of-way 200 feet in width alongside the road. He ended his remarks: "The Club has thus secured a total of $327,602 which has gone directly into the purchase and betterment of the Park."

Praise for Hill's work came from many sources and was abundant and sincere. One of the best expressions of it was printed in a San Jose paper:

Andrew P. Hill is one of the greatest promotion agents in all California ... Hours, days, weeks, months, years of incessant labor, of talking, begging, pleading, persuading followed, and only now, at this late day does Andrew P. Hill see the nearing of the fruition of all his labors and of those who have fought with him.[8]

Hill's Last Years

The year 1915 may have been the most triumphant year in the life of Andrew P. Hill. Three important events occurred that year—all at the Panama-Pacific Exposition in San Francisco and each involving a special tribute to Hill.

Undoubtedly the most important celebration of the year for Hill was the one on May 18 which marked the completion of the road from Santa Clara County into the Big Basin. He wrote to his long-time friend, Alexander P. Murgotten: "My heart is in the work and always shall be."[1]

The second event at the Exposition to concern Hill was the "Pioneer and Old Settlers Day" celebration held October 16. Hill had served as Secretary of the California Pioneers of Santa Clara County for several years. It was in this capacity that he joined six other local men to serve on the committee to plan for the celebration at the Exposition. Letters went out to all pioneer organizations in the state urging all people who had come to California between the years 1846 and 1860 to meet at the Exposition and join in the event:

To the efforts of the Pioneer we owe the organization, birth and development of our beloved California. California, with her incomparable climate, California standing for all that is true, noble and uplifting in civilization, California, with her giant trees, majestic waterfalls, and beautiful mountain scenery, California, with her grand Mission Churches, lifting their spires to the heavens, and dedicated to the service of God, California, with her great

Hill's photo of California Pioneers of Santa Clara County outing in Alum Rock Park. (San Jose Historical Museum)

Crossing the Plains in '49, *painted by Hill in 1915. The painting was purchased by subscription in 1920 and presented to the State of California. At present it hangs in the State Capitol Building, Sacramento.* (Courtesy of Sourisseau Academy, San Jose State University)

educational institutions, offering their culture to the world, California, with her mines of gold, silver and copper; her rich, well-tilled valleys, with their prosperous cities and towns, vine clad hills and lovely mountain homes; all these, with her splendid development of railroads, highways and automobile drives, are primarily due to the energy, labor and wisdom of the California Pioneers and their descendants. Is there any class of people more deserving of a day at the Exposition than the Pioneers?[2]

Hill, given the honor of calling the celebration to order, remarked that it was "probably the largest assemblage of early Californians that has ever been brought together in this State."[3]

The third tribute to Hill that year was the acclaim given his painting, *Crossing the Plains in '49.* Although he had begun

COPYRIGHT OFFICE OF THE UNITED STATES OF AMERICA

Library of Congress—Washington

CERTIFICATE OF COPYRIGHT REGISTRATION

This is to certify, in conformity with section 55 of the Act to Amend a
consolidate the Acts respecting Copyright approved March 4, 1909, that
photograph or other identifying reproduction of the *painting*

named herein has been deposited in th
office under the provisions of the said Act, and that registration for cop
ght for the first term of 28 years has been duly made in the name

[OVER]

Andrew Putnam Hill,
1350 Sherman St., San Jose, Cal.
Crossing the Plains in '49. Size 6½ x 10 fee
ng train of conestoga wagons; one in foreground dr
oxen. Two men walking with dog, two on horse
By Andrew Putnam Hill, of the United States
opy received Feb. 17, 1915. Entry: Class G, XXc., No. 4913

[SEAL]

Thorwald Solb
Register of Copyright

Copyright issued to Hill for his painting, Crossing the Plains in '49. *(Author's Collection)*

Letterhead for the Andrew P. Hill Art Committee which solicited funds to purchase his Crossing the Plains *for the state of California.* (Author's Collection)

the work on the seven by ten foot canvas two years prior to the Exposition, the task of securing the right-of-way for the Saratoga Gap road into Big Basin had prevented him from finishing the painting in time to enter it for judging. He did complete the canvas in February of 1915, securing a United States copyright for the work on February 17, and then placed it on exhibit in the California Building at the Exposition. This painting was Hill's tribute to the California pioneers; the tragic death of his own father after the hardships of the overland journey was his inspiration.

> "Crossing the Plains" reincarnates and perpetuates the spirit of adventure, the indomitable courage, the indifference to hardship, the dogged purpose and the idealistic vision which spurred men and women to give up the comforts and culture of civilization and blaze a trail to unknown homes and through untold dangers.[4]

While the painting could not win an award, it did win approval of Hill's many friends and associates and made the artist feel that his chosen profession was worthwhile, though often unprofitable. In 1920, members of the Sempervirens Club joined with the California Pioneers of Santa Clara County and the Native Sons and Daughters of the Golden West to form an "Andrew P. Hill Art Committee" to solicit funds to purchase the painting for the state. Although the value placed on the work was $15,000, only $3,500 was collected in public subscription. Hill accepted the offer, and on April 23, 1921, the painting was presented to the state during festivities at the Capital National Bank in Sacramento. Governor W. D. Stephens attended, accepting Hill's work for the people of California. At present *Crossing the Plains in '49* hangs in the State Capitol Building in Sacramento.

Problems that emerged as the Big Basin park opened to the public seemed to fall to Hill for solution. From 1913 until his

Hill's photo of the Saratoga Gap road was one of the most popular of the photos sold to tourists. (Author's Collection)

Andrew P. Hill at the foot of the Father Tree in Big Basin Redwoods State Park, c. 1920. (Courtesy of Sempervirens Fund, Inc.)

Below, Saratoga Gap road into Big Basin, built in time for the Panama-Pacific Exposition in San Francisco in 1915. (Courtesy of Sempervirens Fund, Inc.)

Hill painting The Automobile Tree *in 1914.* (Courtesy Sourisseau Academy, San Jose State University)

Hill with his painting, Father of the Forest, *1914.* (Author's Collection)

Hill's studio at Big Basin, completed in May 1918.
(Courtesy Sourisseau Academy)

View of Smith's Creek Hotel on the road to Lick Observatory.
(Courtesy of San Jose Historical Museum)

death in 1922, Hill corresponded regularly on matters per-
taining to the park with State Senator Herbert C. Jones of San
Jose. Senator Jones' mother had been a member of the original
exploration party into the Big Basin in May 1900, and the
Senator proved himself many times to be a friend to Hill and
to the wishes of the Sempervirens Club. He wrote the Saratoga Gap road legislative bill in 1913, and in 1917 introduced
a successful bill to the California State Legislature which
appropriated $150,000 to purchase additional land contiguous
to the California Redwood Park. Senator Jones also served as
an officer of the Sempervirens Club for many years, first as
Secretary and then President, and spent time during his retirement years lecturing to various local groups on the history of
Big Basin.

One major concern of everyone interested in Big Basin was
the threat of forest fire. The disastrous fire in 1904 had left a
vivid impression of what could happen. Hill was in the Basin
when a fire started there in 1916. His account depicted the
event graphically:

Every canyon was full of smoke, the valley was filled,
and some went to sea. Then from a low, smoky, hot
atmosphere, without wind, there appeared through the
rifts of smoke high clouds which seemed to be still at first

Left, Hill at Ingomar Consolidated Gold Mining Company—another financial disaster for the family. (Courtesy of Sourisseau Academy, San Jose State University)

Below, a receipt for stock assessment for the Ingomar Consolidated Gold Mining Co. when Hill was serving as president. (Author's Collection)

Ingomar Consolidated Gold Mining Co.
Room 54, Auzerais Building, San Jose, Cal.,

Received of _Conrad Meyer_
Seven and 72/00 Dollars, $ _7.72_
for Assessment Number One on Certificates _235-256_
Number Shares _717_ Assessment $ _7.17_ cents at $7.72
Edward G. Fuller Secretary

and then to be coming slowly from the South. First sheet lightening afar, then, the low rumble of distant thunder—louder and more lightening ... Then the rain began to pour. It came in torrents and the giant redwoods were saved for that awful fire got an awful swat from the breath of the Almighty who blew it and spat upon it 'till it hid its face and was not.[5]

In 1916 the Redwood Park Commissioners decided to put up a rustic studio in the park for Hill. This was to be the first unit of a park museum. Hill's son, Andrew, Jr., an architect, drew the plans for a sixteen by twenty foot building which would

The letterhead used by Hill for his business.
(Author's Collection)

Left, a bank deposit slip used by Hill in 1913.
(Author's Collection)

serve as a concession stand for film and postcards for tourists and would house Hill's paintings and photographs of the area which were for sale. Included in the plans was a darkroom which would contain developing tanks and an enlarger. Before the studio was finished in May 1918, it had been necessary for Hill to take his photographs during the weekends at the Basin and then return to his home in San Jose to develop them. The new facilities at the park eased his work considerably.

While much of Hill's time at Big Basin was spent working on the problems of the park and taking photographs of the area, there was also time for pleasurable activities. In September 1919, the Sempervirens Club presented a forest play, *The Soul of the Sequoia*, at the park. The author, Don W. Richards, and musical composer, Thomas V. Cator, were both local men. Over five thousand people attended the production, which was staged at the foot of a giant redwood tree in

Hill with California poet Edwin Markham. (Courtesy Sourisseau Academy, San Jose State University)

a natural amphitheater. The play consisted of a prologue, four episodes, and an epilogue.

The first episode was in the form of a dance pantomime typifying the awakening of life. The second was in the cantata form, showing the sowing of the seed of forest life. Grand opera was the third—Indian in theme—which told of the death of Sequoia, the spirit of the forest. The last was the saving of the trees from the axe of the woodsman. Among the leading actors was one of the mountain deer, which, lured by the calls of the assistant park warden, had been tamed sufficiently for the appearance in the play.[6]

The play was shown again the following year on July 3. Richards was again in charge of the production and was joined by Howard Hanson, head of the Music Department of College of the Pacific in San Jose. It had been planned by the Sempervirens Club to have the forest play become an annual event, but a new production, *The Spirit of the Sempervirens*, by Grace

News of the death of Andrew P. Hill appeared on the front page of the San Jose Mercury Herald *on September 4, 1922.* (Author's Collection)

Hyde Trine of Los Gatos, had to be cancelled in 1921 because of lack of monetary support.

By June 1922, Hill's health was causing concern to his family. He was given treatment for a possible heart condition by a doctor in San Jose. On August 15 he and his wife returned to the Basin and remained there until August 29, when his health again deteriorated. They traveled to Pacific Grove to seek treatment from Dr. A. T. Noe, who specialized in the electronic methods of Dr. Albert Abrams. Hill was given radio vibrations which were applied to his lungs, heart, liver and stomach. His wife wrote to her relatives in San Jose:

> The doctor says his condition is so doubtful that it will be necessary to give him all the vibrations he can *stand*, hence the long treatments . . . the result is doubtful. We may be *too late*. I would not be willing to spend all of this money, if it were not a matter of life and death . . . . He never smiles now, so you may know he is pretty sick.[7]

The treatment did not prove successful and Hill died early in the morning on September 3, 1922, at the age of sixty-nine. His

Florence Hill at the Hill Memorial Drinking Fountain, dedicated May 30, 1924 by the Sempervirens Club at Big Basin. (Courtesy Sourisseau Academy, San Jose State University)

last words were reported to be: "Florence, I don't want to die! This is too soon. I have work to do."[8]

Hill's body was taken to San Jose and his funeral was held on September 5 at the San Jose Undertaking Company. The service was a simple but impressive one in which members of the California Pioneers of Santa Clara County participated. Tributes were given by Dr. Charles Pease, pastor of the Unitarian Church, and ex-United States Congressman E. A. Hayes, a friend of Hill for more than thirty years. Following the services, the body was taken to San Francisco for cremation, after which the ashes were taken to Big Basin.

Dedication of
Andrew P. Hill Memorial Tablet
and Fountain

Memorial Day, May 30, 1924
Exercises at Campfire Governor's Camp, 11 a. m.
California Redwood Park

PROGRAM

SENATOR HERBERT C. JONES, Chairman

Solo—Celina Combatalade—"The Trees."

Remarks—Rev. Father Maher, Member Redwood Park Commission.

Remarks—Mrs. Louise C. Jones, Charter Member Sempervirens Club.

Remarks—Mr. A. P. Murgotten, Secretary Sempervirens Club.

Poem—Written by Mrs. W. C. Kennedy to be read by Mrs. John E. Richards.

Remarks—Hon. John E. Richards, Judge State Supreme Court.

Music—"Hymn to Sequoia."

Presentation of Memorial by Hon. Wm. R. Flint, President Sempervirens Club.

Acceptance by Prof. Wing, Vice-Chairman Redwood Park Commission.

—::—

At conclusion of exercises audience will adjourn to fountain to view unveiling of fountain and tablet.

—::—

Wreath presented by Vendome Parlor, Native Daughters of the Golden West

—::—

Wreath presented by California Pioneers of Santa Clara County

Program for the dedication of the Hill Memorial Fountain at Big Basin, May 30, 1924. (Author's Collection)

And Andrew Hill, who loved the big trees so greatly, and so well, is to sleep his long sleep enshrined within one of the forest monarchs, his monument the towering shaft of a living, growing sequoia.[9]

Eleven years before his death, Hill had written his will, using stationery from the Ingomar Consolidated Gold Mining Company. He left all his property to his wife, Florence W. Hill, adding that he had "complete confidence in her judgment." [10] There was not much need for worry, however, as his estate was valued at less than $900. The man who "saved the redwoods" for mankind was unable, in his lifetime of humanitarian pursuits, to amass any kind of a fortune to leave to his family. He did leave them a monument, though, the California Redwood Park, for "in truth it can be said that the Big Basin park is the elongated shadow of Andrew P. Hill."[11]

At rededication of Hill Memorial Drinking Fountain on July 14, 1946, left to right: Herbert C. Jones, Bert Werder, Harriet Weaver, Mrs. Clark Bradley, Mrs. Edmund Brown, R. E. Burton, Clyde Arbuckle, George D. Cress, Everett Powell and Charles L. Cushing. (Courtesy San Jose Historical Museum)

Epilogue

Fifty-six years have passed since the death of Andrew Putnam Hill. It has been seventy-eight years since that first exploration party of interested people went into the Big Basin. Tributes to the work of Hill and the Sempervirens Club live on, in the city of San Jose as well as within the park itself. The Sempervirens Club erected a memorial drinking fountain in a tribute to Hill. The stone fountain was dedicated at the park on May 30, 1924. Some years later it had to be moved when park improvements were made by Civilian Conservation Corps workers. The Park Commissioners arranged for a new drinking fountain of redwood logs to be placed near the "Father Tree," and re-dedication exercises were held July 14, 1946. The Sempervirens Club also planted a row of Sempervirens Redwoods at Backesto Park on North Thirteenth Street in San Jose; one of the trees planted was in honor of Hill. Perhaps the greatest tribute to the man and his work occurred in 1956 when the name "Andrew P. Hill High School" was chosen for a new school built in southeast San Jose.

While all of the above tributes to the memory of Hill are impressive, the fact remains that few people today realize why he has been memorialized. This may be due in part to the American definition of success and individual importance. Americans tend to define both primarily in monetary terms— the acquisition of material goods, the accumulation of wealth and professional or social standing. By these standards, Hill's life was neither successful nor important. His life and career included many ups and downs. He was not a member of the social elite by birth or through professional or financial achievement, and he was not well known outside the boundaries of Santa Clara County. However, success may be viewed in other ways; Hill's importance to history can be measured by his achievements for humanity. Although not a humanitarian in the sense of being a philanthropist, he saw a need and directed his energies toward a singular goal—that of saving a part of the coast redwoods for posterity.

John Muir presented his conservation ideas in national magazines; Hill chose to inform the people of his generation of the need to preserve the coast redwoods through the columns of the local newspapers. He was a man of deeds and deserves no less a place in the history of the conservation movement than does Muir. Andrew P. Hill wanted to preserve the beauty of the Big Basin for posterity, and by diligent effort, he succeeded. He gave his life to Big Basin. He did, indeed, "Save the Redwoods."

Appendix
Known Paintings by Andrew P. Hill

Work	Year Painted	Present Location
Residence of John Wohl, Yolo County	1873	California State Library, Sacramento
"A California Harvest Scene"	1875	Unknown
"Trees at Hotel de Redwood"	1877	Unknown
"The Murphy Party"	1878	Destroyed 1906 Earthquake
"Mission Santa Clara"	1878	Orradre Library, University of Santa Clara
"Camp of Israel"	1882	Unknown
"The Alameda"	1883	San Jose Historical Museum
"Cows in a Meadow"	1883	Society of California Pioneers, San Francisco
"Bridal Veil Falls, Yosemite"	1884	Unknown
Lake Scene	1887	Pat Patterson, Los Gatos
Pasture Scene (oil on wood)	1887	San Jose Historical Museum
"Mission Church"	1889	San Jose Historical Museum
"Driving the Golden Spike"	1906	Destroyed 1906 Earthquake
"Horse Car on the Alameda"	1906	Destroyed 1906 Earthquake

Hill's painting, The Murphy Party. *Painted in 1878, it was awarded a gold medal for best oil painting in landscape at the California State Fair in 1890.* (Courtesy Sourisseau Academy, San Jose State University)

Hill's painting, Rodeo on the San Felipe Ranch, 1909. (Courtesy Sourisseau Academy, San Jose State University)

Left, Hill's painting of Mission Santa Clara as it looked in 1849. He worked from an old daguerreotype taken from an angle which made the window of the baptistry appear to be an arched doorway; thus the usually accurate Hill painted the Mission with two doorways instead of one. (Archives, University of Santa Clara)

Title	Date	Location
"Laying the Cornerstone of Stanford University"	1906	Destroyed 1906 Earthquake
"Rodeo on the San Felipe Ranch"	1909	Fenton O'Connell, San Juan Bautista
"Yosemite Valley"	1910	Mrs. Horace Laughlin, Railroad Flat
"The Father Tree, Big Basin"	1914	Andrew P. Hill High School
"The Automobile Tree"	1914	Unknown
"Crossing the Plains in '49" (original sketch)	1915	San Jose Historical Museum
"Crossing the Plains in '49"	1915	California State Capitol, Sacramento
"Tulare Butte"	1917	San Jose Historical Museum
"Crossing the Plains in '49" (small copy for fund-raising campaign)	1920	Unknown
"The American River Canyon"	1920	Mrs. Horace Laughlin, Railroad Flat
"The American River Canyon" (copy for railroad)	1920	Unknown
"Bull's Head"	1920	San Jose Historical Museum
"Auto Tree" (unfinished)	1922	Sempervirens Fund, Los Altos
"Farney's Garden"	Unknown	Miss Julia Farney, San Jose
"Leland Stanford, Jr.'s Dog"	Unknown	Leland Stanford, Jr., Museum, Stanford Univ.
Dog – "Rover"	Unknown	Andrew P. Hill High School
View of San Francisco As It Was in 1857	Unknown	California State Library, Sacramento
"Sierra Peaks"	Unknown	Society of California Pioneers, San Francisco

SCENE FROM "THE SOUL OF SEQUOIA."

This photo, with frame, was sold at Big Basin as a souvenir of the play presented in 1919, The Soul of the Sequoia. (Author's Collection)

Hill's portrait of Martin Murphy, Jr., 1878. A member of the first emigrant party to ascend Sunset Pass from Donner Lake, in 1844, Murphy at one time held property which later became the city of Sunnyvale. (Courtesy Sunnyvale Historical Society and Museum Association)

Portraits

Martin Murphy, Jr.	1878	Sunnyvale Historical Museum
Ex-Governor Romualdo Pacheco	1878	Unknown
Ex-Governor Newton Booth	1878	Unknown
Governor William Irwin	1878	Unknown
Judge Lawrence Archer	1878	San Jose Historical Museum
Henry B. Wempe	1878	Mrs. Marie Pellerano, San Jose
Anna Maria Wempe	1878	Mrs. Marie Pellerano, San Jose
Nevada Ex-Governor Henry Blasdel	1879	Nevada State Capitol, Carson City
Nevada Ex-Governor Lewis Bradley	1879	Nevada State Capitol, Carson City
Pedro Pacheco	1880	California Historical Society, San Francisco
Judge David Belden	1880	San Jose Historical Museum
Lona Ryder	1883	Mrs. P. Thompson, San Jose
Florence Rock – "Little Girl Blue"	1886	M. H. de Young Memorial Museum, San Francisco
Isaac Branham	1886	Society of California Pioneers, San Francisco
3 Portraits: Tom Rea, Ed Rea, Jim Rea	1886	Patterson's Antiques, Los Gatos (for sale, $3,000)
Mary Hayes-Chynoweth	1914	Mrs. Loy Hayes, San Jose
Mary Hayes-Chynoweth	1915	Mr. Henry Hayes, Grass Valley

Watercolors (Gouache)

"Garden at Edenvale"	1914	Sourisseau Academy, San Jose State Univ.
"Scene on the Murphy Ranch"	1915	Sourisseau Academy, San Jose State Univ.
Residence of Francis Smith, North San Juan	Unknown	San Jose Historical Museum

Notes

Introduction

1. John Muir, *Our National Parks* (Boston: Houghton Mifflin Company, 1901), 364.
2. Ibid., 331.

Chapter One

1. Frank E. Hill and Florence W. Hill, *The Acquisition of California Redwood Park* (San Jose: Privately Printed, 1927), 13.
2. Letter, Andrew P. Hill to Frank E. Hill, May 28, 1917 (Frank Ernest Hill Collection, Manuscripts Collections, Stanford University Library).
3. Robert O'Brien, "The Oil Paintings and the World's Record." San Francisco *Chronicle*, May 21, 1952, "Riptides," 895.
4. "California Artists' Biographies: Andrew P. Hill" (California State Library, Sacramento).
5. Palo Alto *Times*, January 8, 1893, 3.
6. *The Pacific Tree and Vine*, June 30, 1899, 37.

Chapter Two

1. Arthur A. Taylor, *California Redwood Park: An Appreciation* (Sacramento: Superintendent of State Printing, 1912), 12.
2. C. F. Holder, "How a Forest Fire Was Extinguished With Wine," *The Wide World Magazine*, July 1900, 339.
3. Frank E. Hill and Florence W. Hill, *The Acquisition of California Redwood Park* (San Jose: Privately Printed, 1927), 10-11.
4. Josephine Clifford McCrackin, "How the Big Basin Redwoods Were Saved," *Out West*, January 1904, 41.
5. Hill and Hill, *The Acquisition*, 18.
6. Boulder Creek *Mountain Echo*, May 26, 1900, 2. Author's Note:

Hill must have been lost in the Basin at least long enough for his friends to spread the alarm. All were perhaps embarrassed by the incident and played it down when visited by the editor of the Boulder Creek paper.

7. Taylor, *California Redwood Park*, 34-35.

8. Josephine Clifford McCrackin, "About the Big Basin," *Overland Monthly*, August 1900, 135, 139.

Chapter Three

1. Frank E. Hill and Florence W. Hill, *The Acquisition of California Redwood Park* (San Jose: Privately Printed, 1927), 20-21.

2. Thomas A Jacobs, "A History of the Acquisition of the Big Basin as a State Park, 1902" (History 4031 Paper, California State University, Hayward, rev. 1972), 12-13.

3. Hill and Hill, *The Acquisition*, 20-22.

4. Letter, Herbert C. Jones, Sempervirens Club, to Henry C. Jensen, Principal, Andrew P. Hill High School, December 5, 1960.

5. D. M. Delmas, *Speeches and Addresses* (San Francisco: A. M. Robertson, 1901), 363.

6. Arthur A. Taylor, *California Redwood Park: An Appreciation* (Sacramento: Superintendent of State Printing, 1912), 36.

7. David Starr Jordan, *The Days of a Man; Being Memories of a Naturalist, Teacher and Minor Prophet of Democracy, Volume I: 1851-1899* (Yonkers, New York: World Book Company, 1922), 519.

8. Raymond C. Clar, *California Government and Forestry from Spanish Days until the Creation of the Department of Natural Resources in 1927* (Sacramento: State of California, Department of Natural Resources, Division of Forestry, 1959), 181.

9. William R. Dudley, ed., "Forestry Notes," *Sierra Club Bulletin*, June 1901, 337.

10. Theodore Roosevelt, *California Addresses* (San Francisco: The California Promotion Committee, 1903), 70.

11. Santa Cruz *Surf*, March 29, 1901, 2.

Chapter Four

1. Boulder Creek *Mountain Echo*, June 1, 1901, 1.

2. *Mountain Echo*, August 10, 1901, 2-3.

3. Josephine Clifford McCrackin, "In the Heart of the Big Basin

with the Sempervirens Club," *Western Field*, November 1904, 286-291.

4. George Wharton James, "The Romantic History of Josephine Clifford McCrackin," reprinted in Josephine Clifford McCrackin, *The Woman Who Lost Him and Tales of the Army Frontier* (Pasadena, California: George Wharton James, 1913), 41.

5. San Francisco *Chronicle*, January 15, 1908.

6. Frank E. Hill and Florence W. Hill, *The Acquisition of California Redwood Park* (San Jose: Privately Printed, 1927), 35-36.

Chapter Five

1. Letter, Andrew P. Hill to Endora Garonette, Chief, California Historical Department, California State Library, Sacramento, March 25, 1907, 1-2.

2. Franklin Hichborn, *California Politics, 1891-1939, Volume I* (Los Angeles: J. R. Haynes Foundations, 1957-1961), 505-509.

3. Letter, Florence W. Hill to Frank E. Hill, February 9, 1917 (Frank Ernest Hill Collection, Manuscripts Collections, Stanford University Library).

4. Letter, Andrew P. Hill to Frank E. Hill, January 19, 1918.

5. Circular Letter, "Greater California Redwood Park for 1915," by order Sempervirens Club, Andrew P. Hill, President, n.d. (Sempervirens Club Collection, San Jose Historical Museum).

6. Frank E. Hill and Florence W. Hill, *The Acquisition of California Redwood Park* (San Jose: Privately Printed, 1927), 41-42.

7. "Sempervirens Club at Banquet, Celebrates Big Appropriation," San Jose *Mercury Herald*, June 22, 1913, 8.

8. Hill and Hill, *The Acquisition*, 47-49.

Chapter Six

1. Letter, Andrew P. Hill to Alexander P. Murgotten, January 10, 1912 (Andrew P. Hill Collection, San Jose Historical Museum).

2. Letter, "My Dear Sir," signed by Alex P. Murgotten, Chairman, Andrew P. Hill, Secretary, Pioneer and Old Settlers Day Committee, September 7, 1915 (Andrew P. Hill Collection, San Jose Historical Museum).

3. *A Souvenir of Pioneer and Old Settler's Day, Panama-Pacific Exposition*, October 16, 1915 (California State Library, Sacramento).

4. Andrew P. Hill, "How I Came to Paint 'Crossing the Plains'," 1-2 (Andrew P. Hill Collection, San Jose Historical Museum).

5. Letter, Andrew P. Hill to Frank E. Hill, September 24, 1916 (Frank Ernest Hill Collection, Manuscripts Collections, Stanford University Library).

6. Eugene T. Sawyer, *History of Santa Clara County, California with Biographical Sketches of the Leading Men and Women of the County Who Have Been Identified with its Growth and Development from the Early Days to the Present* (Los Angeles: Historic Record Company, 1922), 209-10.

7. Letter, Florence W. Hill to Andrew P. Hill, Jr., September 1, 1922 (Andrew P. Hill Collection, San Jose Historical Museum).

8. B. H. Laughlin, "Trees of Enchantment; the Ever-Living," 24, Archives, Big Basin Redwoods State Park.

9. San Jose *Mercury Herald*, September 5, 1922, 9; September 6, 1922, 11.

10. Last Will and Testament, Andrew P. Hill, dated September 2, 1911, Probate Records, Santa Clara County Recorder.

11. Bertha Marguerite Rice, *Builders of Our Valley; A City of Small Farms*, Vol. 1 (San Jose: Privately Printed, 1957), 227.

Reference Sources

Unpublished Works

Andrew P. Hill High School. San Jose, California. Andrew P. Hill File, Library.

Big Basin Redwoods State Park. Big Basin, California. Archives.

Bronson, Crevola. *When Santa Clara County Was Young*. Series of articles by Mrs. Fremont Older, "In the Evening News."

California State Library. Sacramento, California. "California Artists' Biographies."

California State Library. Sacramento, California. Andrew P. Hill Collection.

Death Certificate. Santa Clara County, California. Baby Boy Hill, February 8, 1884.

Delayed Certificate of Birth. Sacramento, California. Department of Public Health. Bureau of Vital Statistics. Frank Ernest Hill, November 30, 1943.

1850 Census. Porter County, Indiana.

Grantee Files. Amador County, California. Recorder's Office.

Hill, Andrew P., Jr. "Memories of Early Days at Big Basin." Mrs. Horace R. Laughlin, Railroad Flat, California. Private Collection. Hill Family Papers.

Jacobs, Thomas A. "A History of the Acquisition of the Big Basin as a State Park, 1902." History 4031 Paper, California State University, Hayward. Rev. 1972.

Jones, Herbert C. "History of the Acquisition of the Big Basin as a State Park." Bancroft Library. University of California. Berkeley, California.

Laughlin, B. H. "Trees of Enchantment; the Ever-Living." Big Basin Redwoods State Park. Big Basin, California. Archives.

Laughlin, Mrs. Horace R. Railroad Flat, California. Private Collection. Hill Family Papers.

————. Railroad Flat, California. Private Collection. Rose Family Papers.

Marriage License. Amador County, California. Albert H. Rose to Catharine Barry, December 31, 1862.

Marriage License. Porter County, Indiana. Elijah Putnam Hill to Jane A. Rose, April 2, 1850.

Marriage License. Santa Clara County, California. Andrew Putnam Hill to Florence Maria Watkins, April 3, 1883.

Probate Records. Santa Clara County, California. Andrew P. Hill.

San Jose Historical Museum. San Jose, California. Andrew P. Hill Collection.

San Jose Historical Museum. San Jose, California. Sempervirens Club Collection.

Sourisseau Academy for California State and Local History. Department of History, San Jose State University. San Jose, California. Andrew P. Hill, Jr., Collection.

Stanford University Library. Stanford, California. Manuscripts Collections. Frank Ernest Hill Collection.

Stanford University Library. Stanford, California. Manuscripts Collections. Herbert C. Jones Collection.

Superior Court Defendants Index. Santa Clara County, California. Hill and Yard, October 3, 1894.

Published Works:

Adams, Kramer. *The Redwoods*. New York: Popular Library, Inc., n.d.

Anderson, Buell D. "A California Conservationist." *Sunset Magazine*. July 1914, 118-20.

"Andrew P. Hill, Artist and Photographer." *The Pacific Tree and Vine*. June 30, 1899, 37.

Big Basin Redwoods State Park. Sacramento: State of California, The Resources Agency, Department of Parks and Recreation, n.d.

Bishop's Oakland Directory for 1877-1878, Containing a Business Directory, Street Guide, a Correct Map of the City, Together with a Record of the City Government, its Institutions, etc., Also a Directory of the Town of Alameda. San Francisco: B. C. Vandall, 1877.

Busch, Noel F. *T. R.; The Story of Theodore Roosevelt and His Influence on Our Times*. New York: Reynal and Company, 1963.

California Polk-Husted Directory Company's San Jose City and Santa Clara County Directory, 1907-1908, Comprising an Alphabetically Arranged List of Business and Professional Men, Firms, Corporations and Private Citizens, Where Located and Telephone Numbers, with an Improved Street Guide, a Revised Map of the City, a Miscellaneous Directory, State, City and County Officers, Terms of Court, Public and Private Schools, and Benevolent Societies, and a Complete Classified Business Directory. San Jose: Eaton and Company Press, 1907.

California School of Design: San Francisco Institute of Art Affiliated with the University of California; Circular of Information Regarding Instruction in Drawing, Painting, Decorative Designing, Modeling, Illustrating and Teacher's Course. San Francisco: The San Francisco Art Association, n.d.

Clar, Raymond C. *California Government and Forestry from Spanish Days until the Creation of the Department of Natural Resources in*

1927. Sacramento: State of California, Department of Natural Resources, Division of Forestry, 1959.

Colusa County Historical Society. *Wagon Wheels*. August 1951, 1-3.

Delmas, D. M. *Speeches and Addresses*. San Francisco: A. M. Robertson, 1901.

Directory of the City of San Jose, for 1878, Containing a General Register of the Names of All Residents, and a Classified Business Directory, Together with a Historical Sketch of the City, a General Review of its Progress, and a Variety of Statistical Information, Also a Directory of Santa Clara, Containing a General Register of Names. San Jose: Cottle and Wright, Printers, 1878.

Directory of the City of San Jose, for 1887. San Jose: Cottle and Wright, Printers, 1887.

Directory of the City of San Jose, for 1890. San Jose: Cottle and Wright, Printers, 1890.

Directory of the City of San Jose, for 1892. San Jose: Cottle and Wright, Printers, 1892.

Directory of the City of San Jose, for 1895. San Jose: Cottle and Wright, Printers, 1895.

Directory of the City of San Jose, for 1898-1899. San Jose: Cottle and Wright, Printers, 1898.

Dudley, William R., ed. "Forestry Notes." *Sierra Club Bulletin*. February 1901, 262-70; June 1901, 336-39.

Final Calendar of Legislative Business, California Legislature, 1901. Sacramento, n.p., 1901.

Final Report of the California World's Fair Commission, Including a Description of all Exhibits from the State of California, Collected and Maintained Under Legislation Enactments, at the World's Columbian Exposition, Chicago, 1893. Sacramento: State Printing Office, 1894.

Frome, Michael. *Whose Woods These Are: The Story of the National*

Forests. Garden City, N.Y.: Doubleday and Company, Inc., 1962.

Graham, Frank, Jr. *Man's Dominion: The Story of Conservation in America.* New York: M. Evans and Company, Inc., 1971.

Guinn, J. M. *History of the State of California and Biographical Record of Coast Counties, California.* Chicago: The Chapman Publishing Company, 1904.

Hichborn, Franklin. *California Politics, 1891-1939.* Vol. 1. Los Angeles: J. R. Haynes Foundations, 1957-1961.

Hill, Frank E. and Florence W. Hill. *The Acquisition of California Redwood Park.* San Jose: Privately Printed, 1927.

Holder, C. F. "How a Forest Fire Was Extinguished with Wine." *The Wide World Magazine.* July 1900, 338-48.

Hoover, Mildred Brooks. *Historic Spots in California Counties of the Coast Range.* Stanford: Stanford University Press, 1937.

Jones, Holway R. *John Muir and the Sierra Club: The Battle for Yosemite.* San Francisco: Sierra Club, 1965.

Jordan, David Starr. *The Days of a Man; Being Memories of a Naturalist, Teacher and Minor Prophet of Democracy, Volume One: 1851-1899.* Yonkers, N.Y.: World Book Company, 1922.

Koch, Margaret. *Santa Cruz County: Parade of the Past.* Fresno, Cal.: Valley Publishers, 1973.

Leydet, Francois. *The Last Redwoods and the Parkland of Redwood Creek.* San Francisco: Sierra Club, 1969.

McCrackin, Josephine Clifford. "How the Big Basin Redwoods Were Saved." *Out West.* January 1904, 32-44.

————. "In the Heart of the Big Basin with the Sempervirens Club." *Western Field.* November 1904, 285-92.

————. *The Woman Who Lost Him and Tales of the Army Frontier.* Pasadena, Cal.: George Wharton James, 1913.

McHenry, Robert, ed., with Charles Van Doren. *A Documentary History of Conservation in America.* New York: Praeger Publishers, 1972.

Mars, Amaury. *Reminiscences of Santa Clara Valley and San Jose with the Souvenir of the Carnival of Roses Held in Honor of the Visit of President McKinley, Santa Clara County, California, May 13-14-15, 1901.* San Francisco: Artistic Publishing Company, 1901.

Muir, John. *Our National Parks.* Boston: Houghton Mifflin Company, 1901.

Pinchot, Gifford. *Breaking New Ground.* New York: Harcourt, Brace and Company, 1947.

————. *The Fight for Conservation.* New York: Doubleday, Page and Company, 1910.

Report XIV of the State Mineralogist: Mines and Mineral Resources of Portions of California. Sacramento: State Printing Office, 1915.

Rice, Bertha Marguerite. *Builders of Our Valley; A City of Small Farms.* Vol 1. San Jose: Privately Printed, 1957.

Richards, Don W. *The Soul of Sequoia; A Forest Play.* San Jose: Hillis-Murgotten Company, 1919.

Rogers, Justus H. *Colusa County, Its History Traced from a State of Nature Through the Early Period of Settlement and Development, to the Present Day with a Description of its Resources, Statistical, Tables, Etc., Also Biographical Sketches of Pioneers and Prominent Residents.* Orland, Cal.: Privately Printed, 1891.

Roosevelt, Nicholas. *Conservation: Now or Never.* New York: Dodd, Mead and Company, 1970.

Roosevelt, Theodore. *An Autobiography.* New York: Charles Scribner's Sons, 1925.

————. *California Addresses.* San Francisco: The California Promotion Committee, 1903.

The San Francisco Directory for the Year Commencing April 1876, Embracing a General Directory of Residents and a Business Directory; Also, a Directory of Streets, Public Offices, etc., and a Reliable Map of the City Together with the Consolidation Act and its Amendments, Officers of the Municipal Government, Societies and Other Organiza-

tions, and a Great Variety of Useful and Statistical Information, Exhibiting at a Glance the Past History and Present Condition of the City. San Francisco: Henry C. Langley, 1876.

The San Francisco Directory for the Year 1882. San Francisco: Henry C. Langley, 1882.

San Jose City Directory, Also Street Guide to the City of San Jose, Together with a Classified Business Directory of the County, 1903-1904. San Jose: F. M. Husted, 1903.

San Jose City Directory, 1904-1905. San Jose: F. M. Husted, 1904.

San Jose City Directory, 1905-1906. San Jose: F. M. Husted, 1905.

San Jose City Directory, 1906-1907. San Jose: F. M. Husted, 1906.

Santa Clara County and its Resources, a Souvenir of the San Jose Mercury. San Jose: Smith and Eaton, 1895.

Santa Clara County Directory, Including the City of San Jose, Giving Name, Occupation and Residence of all Adult Persons in the County. San Jose: L. L. Bettys, Publisher, 1889.

Sawyer, Eugene T. *History of Santa Clara County, California with Biographical Sketches of the Leading Men and Women of the County Who Have Been Identified with its Growth and Developments from the Early Days to the Present.* Los Angeles: Historic Record Company, 1922.

Sempervirens Club of California: Articles of Incorporation and By-Laws, Adopted the Twenty-Eighth of February, One Thousand Nine Hundred and Seven, San Jose, California. San Jose: Press of Henry Murgotten, 1907.

Simpson, Joseph Cairn. "Horses of California, from the Days of the Missions to the Present: Fourth Paper—The Horses of Palo Alto." *Sunset Magazine.* May 1901, 9-23.

A Souvenir of Pioneer and Old Settler's Day, Panama-Pacific Exposition, October 16, 1915. San Jose, n.p., 1915.

The Statutes of California and Amendments to the Codes Passed at the Thirty-Fourth Session of the Legislature, 1913. Sacramento: Friend William Richardson, Superintendent of State Printing, 1913.

The Statutes of California and Amendments to the Codes Passed at the Forty-Second Session of the Legislature, 1917. Sacramento: California Printing Office, 1917.

Taylor, Arthur A. *California Redwood Park: An Appreciation*. Sacramento: Superintendent of State Printing, 1912.

Wagner, Jack R. *Gold Mines of California*. Berkeley: Howell-North Books, 1970.

Walter, Carrie Stevens. "The Preservation of the Big Basin." *Overland Monthly*. October 1902, 354-61.

Weaver, Harriett. "He Saved the Redwoods." *Westways*. January 1954, 25.

Newspapers

Boulder Creek *Mountain Echo*, 1900-1907.

Daily Alta California, February 5, 1878.

New York *Times*, November 4, 1969.

Pacific Rural Press, May 6, 1876.

Palo Alto *Times*, 1893-1901.

Redwood City *Times-Gazette*, 1886-1887.

San Francisco *Bulletin*, January 24, 1901.

San Francisco *Chronicle*, 1900-1908; March 21, 1952.

San Jose *Daily Mercury*, 1901-1913.

San Jose *Daily Morning Times*, April 4, 1883.

San Jose *Herald*, 1900.

San Jose *Mercury*, 1900-1906; April 20, 1956; August 5, 1973.

San Jose *Mercury Herald*, 1913-1934.

Santa Cruz *Morning Sentinel*, June 29, 1901.

Santa Cruz *Sentinel*, 1900; 1952-1968.

Santa Cruz *Surf*, 1901.

Watsonville *Register*, September 27, 1907.

Index

98